Feeding a

Advanced Network Marketing

This is the 3rd Edition of Feeding a Giant

Bob Crisp
10/15/2009

Also by Bob Crisp

Raising a Giant 2.0

Giant Consequences

How to Become a Millionaire in Network Marketing

The Poor Network Marketers Guide to Doing Better

NEW

Social Media and Network Marketing (Spring 2010)

For more go to www.gobobcrisp.com or www.gocrispblog.com

TABLE OF CONTENTS

CHAPTER TWENTY-TWO

CHAPTER TWENTY-THREE

The best way to contact me is by email...

bob@allaxismedia.com or **bobcrisp212@yahoo.com**

MLM
THE STATE
OF THE INDUSTRY
REVISITED

Prelude

"Whatever you do, you need courage. Whatever course you decide upon, there is always someone to tell you you're wrong."

-- Emerson

This is the third edition of "Feeding a Giant" for those who bought a previous version I thank you... please tell your friends and business associates about this one I believe it to be my finest work to date. If you need to reach me you may at... bobcrisp212@yahoo.com or bob@allaxismedia.com.

I no longer seek success as a "distributor" in the industry but have dedicated myself to helping others who share my vision for the future of the industry. You can find my "generic" marketing materials on my website www.gobobcrisp.com . I also have a free networking blog you will find a link on my website and you may subscribe to my FREE ezine too.

My focus today is how the internet and particularly "emarketing" solutions can enhance your global business opportunities. Paul Zane Pilzer in his book "The Next Millionaires" says that "Intellectual Distribution" is the wave of the future... that was in 2005. My hope is to be another set of eyes and ears for you to decipher the complex web of networking solutions as they become available.

I am constantly amazed at the tide of people who join the network marketing industry without any thought of what will be required of them or the consequences involved. No other industry that I know of inspires such naive behavior. People with advanced degrees are no more immune than those without any formal college or advanced training. How can normally intelligent people approach a new career with such hopes and aspiration, and expect to give so little attention to the finer points of a successful endeavor?

In my previous book "Raising a Giant," I discussed "The System" and the key elements in laying the foundation for a successful journey to the top of the network marketing world. In this book I will discuss the details of long-term growth and the pitfalls of ignoring the danger signs posted along the way. I will point out some things you, your company, or upline may not like or have thought of. I will gore some sacred cows and challenge some long held erroneous beliefs.

In our quest for truth we will look long and hard at the reasons why people fail and succeed. Why some companies and organizations retain their distributors longer, get more performance out of the ones they recruit, and why their training systems work better.

There can be no argument that there are some who do better at the job than others. Some successful leaders continue to grow and prosper while the overnight sensations usually falter along the way and are supplanted or removed altogether.

I must first confess that most of what you read here is "stuff" I've learned the hard way. Unfortunately, for me many the lessons found here have been experienced from the wrong side of the fence. Not that my mentors didn't warn me in advance, but simply I was too blind or ignorant to heed the advice. Someone has said that true wisdom can be found in learning from the experience of others. I can vouch for the truth of this statement.

After reading and studying the elements found herein you can no longer say you didn't know. Violate these principles and you will certainly pay dearly. I did!

In four short years I built an organization estimated at around 200,000 downline members. My fourth year downline retail sales figures were over one hundred million dollars! My gross income was over five million dollars. I had a two million dollar jet, ten thousand square foot home, twenty-three cars, two vacation homes, worldwide vacations, and the respect of thousands. Five years later I was bankrupt, couldn't get a loan or phone calls returned. It was devastating!

Dr. Robert Schuler says "Success is never permanent, and failure is never final." I am recovering quite nicely, it has been a long road back and the journey continues. I am writing this to serve as a guide book for those whose dreams are those of a giant, and, who have the ability to see the giant vision of the road ahead. Those who realize the importance of having a road map to follow.

It is not my intention to set myself up as an example to follow but rather as an imperfect model to use as a measuring stick for progress. I have no special talents or magic spell. I dropped out of college after three inglorious semesters and went to work as an aircraft mechanic. I sold Fuller Brush products door-to-door while I was in school, and sold vacuum cleaners for Rexair without success. I entered the Life Insurance industry in 1968 and failed miserably for eighteen months before attending a seminar that changed my life.

My life insurance career took off and I qualified for my company's top clubs and awards for several years. I discovered the good life and the joy that a larger than average income could bring. My first experience in network marketing was an incredible one. After nine years, due to other business failures, I sold my downline business. Today I am a well-paid consultant. I guess when you've done as many things well and wrong as I have, your life becomes a beacon to those whose ships are still at sea.

"Feeding a Giant" is about making the right choices, about taking the correct path when you come to the proverbial "fork in the road." The decisions ahead are many, the opportunities limitless. This book is for those who are visionaries, for leaders, and would-be leaders.

My goal here is to awaken you to the greatness that lies within you. Challenge you to reach your highest and fullest potential as a leader in the most exciting industry ever! To start your creative juices flowing and allow a river of excellence to burst forth from you and flood the world of network marketing with a new generation of focused and determined leaders!

My upline was fond of ending events with the statement "Go and grow," a moving target is harder to hit, and a person is either growing or dying. Say yes to the dreams inside you and then give everything you've got to see them to fruition!

Chapter 1

OBJECTS IN THE MIRROR ARE

CLOSER THAN THEY APPEAR

"The chains of habit are too light to be felt until
they're too heavy to be broken."
-- Emerson

Everyone who owns a car with a right side rear view mirror has seen the words "Objects in the mirror are closer than they appear." The obvious intent is to warn the driver that the mirror's shape has distorted the reflection, and has brought closer to view, things which one should avoid, usually while backing up. In life this would seem to be a good warning as well. It is also possible that the things that have brought you to this juncture of your life may be impacting your vision of the future too much.

It is human nature to carry forward experiences which impact our daily lives. Since entering network marketing in 1975, I've noticed that too many people allow things from their past to hinder them in their progress toward success. Since childhood, we have been told "Don't speak to strangers." Now upon entering network marketing, we are told to meet as many new people as we can! As children we are admonished to "Speak only when spoken to." Now we speak up and connect with others on sight.

Self denigrating statements such as "I've never been good at sales," or "I'm too shy to be good with people," or "I can't say or do this or that," are all learned behavior patterns or characteristics and prove the point that "Objects in the mirror are closer than they appear." We think we've left behind old prejudices and behavior patterns, but in truth we not only bring them with us, we actually defend their merits by placing credence on them in the present tense.

We've been told not to "work too hard," that this might create hypertension or disease in our lives, but the truth is that hard work never did kill anyone. Our lives have been programmed to accept what we read in the newspapers, hear on the radio, or see on television as truth. We have been told that super athletes like Michael Jordan, Tiger Woods, or the legendary Babe Ruth were or are unique people with special gifts, but don't realize that these "gifted athletes" worked extraordinarily hard to make the most of those gifts. Charles Barkley, a super star NBA forward and outspoken advocate of education for inner city youth says, "I may have been given some talent, but I've taken that talent a long way."

I'm convinced that undeveloped or untapped talent lies within each and every one of us. The problem is that we have buried the talent under a pile of mediocrity. Daily proving the point that the "objects in the mirror are closer than they appear."

Just because you haven't had any super successes in your life does not mean that you are incapable of having super success. It may mean that you have not been willing or able, in the past, to apply yourself to an opportunity in such a way as to rise above past failures and accomplishments. Objects in the mirror are closer than they appear.

In this new day of achievement, and in the dawn of personal growth, all past experiences are laid to rest and the light of new opportunities for achievement are at hand.

The challenge of dealing with the past must be looked at from two distinctively different viewpoints. First is the way you look at the past. The second is the way "they" (your future or present downline) look at their past and how this impacts your growth pattern.

You must not let your past predict your future! You must find excitement in learning about your new career and find joy in the process of learning new skills in leadership, marketing, communications, and business in general. This is not a small accomplishment. As the comic strip character Pogo once proclaimed, "We have met the enemy, and he is us." I have often advised people who come into network marketing, to "take the rear view mirrors off," so to speak, and focus almost entirely on the present and future.

One of the most important lessons to be learned early in your career in network marketing is that people do what you do, not what you say. Good advice reminds us that "What parents do in moderation, children do in excess." It ultimately comes down to the issue of priorities. How much importance you place on learning new habits and skills will usually determine how much emphasis your downline will place on those things also.

Most people can't get their businesses off the ground

because their "start up strategy" is so weak that it renders them impotent in motivating others to follow an excellent example. They are unable to lead others to make firm decisions and commitments to "their" businesses. I call this the "Line of perpetual compromise."

Compromise means no one gets what they want in the interest of harmony and "the greater good." I suggest that what is needed is "Collaboration" where good minds come together to come up with the best solutions. Success doesn't happen in a vacuum neither does failure.

Sooner or later, hopefully sooner, one realizes that the business of network marketing is a business which relies solely on the strength of relationships built with your customer base (mainly your downline wholesale customer). Relationship building is not one of the courses most take in high school or college. Therefore most newcomers need to enroll in "Relationship Building 101." This may mean massive doses of new people skills, communication skills, and leadership training.

I personally was successful as a life insurance agent, was the music and youth director at my church, and taught a large young adult Sunday School class, but was lacking basic understanding of how all of this impacted network marketing.

I've found that seminars, meetings, events, audio and video CDs and DVDs, and hundreds of hours of practice will make anyone an effective and successful leader. Chart out your game-plan for personal skill development, and don't spare any expense. This investment is a surefire winner if you apply the knowledge gained. Network marketing is just the right place to gain maximum financial benefit from the investment in your personal growth! Remember, personal worth precedes net worth!

Most new people make the mistake of emphasizing the sale of products as a first step to building a network. While product knowledge and information is vital, the process of "selling" products may expose the weaknesses in someone's arsenal of people skills too quickly. Maybe it would be better to do some remedial training first and get the new person to gain personal familiarity with the product line before sending them out to fight without combat training first.

One must also consider the way past experiences effect the way newcomers in your downline react. It is safe to assume that most new members are ill prepared to deal with the complexities of network marketing. In our desire to make the business simple, (KISS - Keep It Simple Stupid) we have inadvertently failed to make it plain that simple does not mean stupid. That there are some skills and techniques that when deployed properly can make the business easier. It should also be pointed out that telling someone the business is easy may be setting them up for failure.

I personally like Art Williams', founder of A.L. William's Insurance Company (Now Primemerica) approach to building a network marketing business, he says "I'm not telling you it's going to be easy, I'm telling you it's going to be worth it."

Why is it that someone new to network marketing, a person of reasonable intelligence, often will take their new network marketing business opportunity to the most unlikely counselor, usually their brother-in-law, barber or some other profoundly successful advisor, and take their word for the viability of the opportunity?

It astounds me that so much emphasis is placed by broke people on the advice of other broke people. Human nature can be the only explanation. Do people having marriage problems go to people recently divorced to find out how to fix the problem? No. It would be like a thirsty man going to the desert for water, it simply defies logic. Old habits are hard, not impossible, to change. Objects in the mirror are closer than they appear.

There is much you can do to shape the will and way of the newcomer in your downline. A healthy culture will uplift and focus the newcomer on a positive vision of hope and excitement, without burying them in complex strategies, a morass of technical product information or analytical support data.

Logic must be balanced with strong emotional messages of support. Remember a newborn baby isn't challenged to talk or walk, but is fed and nurtured and loved! Newcomers must be made to feel valued and a level of expectation must be created that engenders a spirit of success.

Many people bring positive experiences to network marketing and they can use those experiences to build on. I was a successful insurance agent. There were thousands in my downline that had successful businesses, medical practices, and were highly regarded in their occupations. These positive experiences appear in the mirror too.

The master teacher / leader learn to use these past

experiences as a foundation for excellence in network marketing. It is a mistake however, to conclude that just because someone was successful in another endeavor, that their success wills carry-over into your business!

Each of us brings baggage along with us. I was privileged to be the featured speaker at my high school graduation. (Too many years ago now to recall) My topic was "Let's Pack a Suitcase." Among the things I challenged my classmates to pack their suitcases with were; a positive mental attitude, memories of the good times spent with classmates and friends, lessons learned from caring teachers and coaches, and goals which would challenge them to reach for the stars!

Everyone has excess baggage to deal with. Deal with it and move on. Even though objects in the mirror may seem close, the truth is they are gone. They are over with. They are unchangeable. They are immutable. They are not the total sum of us but merely a reflection of things gone by. The world is going to ask us today, "So what have you done lately?" No one really cares whether you were a roaring success or a miserable failure. Celebrate the new day with a new spirit. If you have successes build on them. If your life has been one disappointment after another, forget it; move on, this is your time to climb!

SUMMARY

1. No one but you has your experience.
2. Only you can change it for the better.
3. Those you follow and those you lead will need your dedication and commitment to be such that success is the only option.

4. Put it behind you and move on. Don't linger, it doesn't pay.

Internet Notes:

   With so much available information available on the internet it is reasonable to expect that an intelligent person would seek out the best intel available before choosing a network marketing company. Take some time to seriously research the strengths and weaknesses of various companies. Pay plans are very different... products may not be what they are purported to be... and most startup companies are poorly financed making them vulnerable to failure.

Chapter 2

FOLLOW THE FEEDER

"Peter, Lovest thou me?" "Yea Lord you know I love you." "Feed my sheep." -- Jesus

I love to eat. Some people eat to live and some live to eat. I think I fall in the second category. Certainly hungry people seek out what they are hungry for. Hungry people do more and with more passion. You don't want to be in the way of someone who is hungry in a buffet line; and in an "all-you-can-eat" smorgasbord, they lose money when I buy a ticket.

If there's one thing I am certain of, it is that every living thing on this planet needs to be fed. The shepherd leads the sheep to green pastures, the good farmer makes certain his livestock has plenty of food and water, the leaders of nations know that their citizens must, above all things, be fed.

Network marketing is about "feeding." It is about "leading by feeding." Meetings get smaller when the food runs out. (Both literally and figuratively) Downlines fail to grow when the nourishment is not available. Company growth is stunted when personal growth ceases. Truly it can be said that "The Feeder is The Leader" or that the "Eater follows the Feeder."

Think about it for a moment. Don't you want to be fed spiritually when you go to church? Fed physically when you go to a restaurant? Then don't you want to be fed great business building ideas and concepts every time you attend a training seminar, meet with someone in your upline, listen to a tape, or read company literature and materials? Certainly you do, and so does everyone else.

Early in my network marketing career, someone gave this morsel of advice, "The sin of the desert, is knowing where the water hole is and not telling anyone." The sin of the network marketing world is knowing what to do and not telling others.

The key to your growth is in knowing where to find what is good and nutritious in a business environment. When you are fed the wrong or insufficient information then the natural tendency is to pass it along to someone else. I call this the "Line of perpetual ignorance." Unfortunately it runs rampant in most of network marketing. (Past experiences create "filters" which can skew and distort the learning process.)

So if the "Feeder is The Leader," then where does the leader learn how to become a feeder? There are many resources. This book and my previous book "Raising a Giant" are but a couple. They are filled with foundational concepts which will put the reader on a course for success. They act similar to a computer operating system which allows the software and the hardware to work together.

I believe that great leaders need to be well informed. That means taking time each day to update yourself on current events, and progress in technology that may impact your future. Every leader should spend time each day doing something to improve themselves. Reading a positive thinking book will help keep you focused on the beauty of every day and every experience.

We started every new distributor out with a copy of "The Magic of Thinking Big" by Dr. David Swartz. Sure we had many who refused to read, but they had a copy anyway. The "Feeder" may not be able to make you eat but they can put food on the table. Weekly and monthly meetings and events... online webinars, conference calls and podcasts need to be filled with information and exciting news.

I always read the paper with a pair of scissors in my hands. Hardly a day goes by that I don't find a human interest story, new statistical data to support a product, or something that uplifts and informs. I saw a story in a recent issue of "Town and Country" magazine that told about new studies on nutrition that would be great reading for anyone who sells health and nutrition products.

I set aside time every day to listen to CDs and DVDs. (Usually in the car). I find that this distracts me from problems or concerns and refocuses me on the solutions. Before meetings I never open mail or deal with negatives, because it may get me off track on what the group needs when I get on stage. Instead, I listen to CDs and DVDs, uplifting music, take a hot shower, review some positive notes that I make to remind me of the evening's objectives.

When I was building my first downline organization, I would say a little prayer on my way from the car to the front door, "Lord help me be the difference for someone here tonight." To me "being the difference" meant feeding those who attended some new insights, sharing life's experiences, dreams and hopes, so that they would be inspired to act immediately to change their lives priorities and focus on becoming a successful part of my downline. If the "Feeder is The Leader," then the reverse must also be true, "The Leader is The Feeder."

A good leader knows just what to feed who, when, where and how much. My father, who was a Baptist minister, had a great story he used to tell about a small town in Oklahoma where it had rained so hard that the town flooded. The only person who could get through the flood for church on Sunday night was one old farmer. Well, the preacher and farmer set and talked until well past time for church to start, the preacher asked the farmer if he thought that he should preach? The farmer said, "Well preacher when I go out to feed my cattle, if only one comes up to eat, I feed him." The preacher accepted the challenge, strode to the pulpit and preached hell fire and damnation for an hour and a half. When he finished he asked the farmer what he thought, the farmer said, "Preacher if only one of my cows comes up to eat, I don't dump the whole load on him."

Being the "Feeder" means knowing what to do and say. It is a large responsibility and is not to be taken lightly. Knowing how to feed those who have "heard it all before" is as important as remembering that some in the audience haven't heard any of it.

Let me give you an example. My book "Raising a Giant" is regarded by some as the best book on network marketing ever! (My mother's opinion is the only one who counts) While I'm flattered and pleased, the fact remains that comparatively few use it in their businesses. They buy the book, read it, gain from it but they don't "recommend it." (sell It to others) go to www.gobobcrisp.com

The art of "feeder duplication" is getting others to do what you do. I have found a direct relationship between the amount of books, and CDs and DVDs sold, and meeting attendance and the sales volume of an organization.

New award winners. New pin winners last month should produce more new pin winners next month, which means a bigger crowd next month. The cycle continues or it ceases. When you take responsibility for the "movement" of information through the sale of books and CDs and DVDs, then your group will start to grow again.

Most companies and upline leaders tend to treat "symptoms" not the disease or reason itself. If your recruiting is down there is a reason and that reason is NOT because people have stopped recruiting! They have stopped recruiting because they have lost courage, focus, and their belief system has been damaged. So teaching them how to "Show the plan" isn't going to cure the recruiting problem is it? They need a good old dose of encouragement... a good, positive CD or a pat on the back by you.

Believe it or not but there is a direct correlation between the movement of personal development tools (books, CDs, and DVDs) and the forward motion of your team.

We measured our future growth by the present purchase of certain tools. Rarely is what you're seeing today a result of what's happening today... rather it is a result of what happened six to eight weeks earlier... a key leader goes on vacation... no tool movement... back orders by the company... checks that are late or wrong... all can slow down or stop progress.

If you moved 50 books last month your goal should be greater than that for this month. You can't sit back and wait for the downline to understand this dynamic. You must "feed" them! Lead them, tell them what you did, and expect them to duplicate you. Until they move 50 books, then they haven't duplicated what you did!

Doesn't it make sense to get five people to do what you did? Order 50 books, get the tape flow going, emphasize to your leaders the importance of each of them knowing exactly how many they had at the meeting last week and to have a real tangible goal of an increase this week. Accountability is essential. Count heads. Know where each person fits in your downline; help those set goals for personal growth. Feed the sheep and the sheep will follow the "feeder."

The Good Book tells us "A sower went forth to sow" it certainly implied that whatever we sow we reap." There is nothing like sowing the good seed. Be prepared, be vigilant, be certain, and be enthusiastic! Be a giant feeder and a giant, hungry crowd will flock to you to be fed!

Who's Hungry?

In an audience of a hundred or so network marketers you have a wide variety of appetites, you have new people just getting started, you have happy people who are experiencing success, you have discouraged distributors who are thinking that it won't work for them, you have negative people who will whine and complain to anyone if given a chance, and so on. How do you deal with so many differing needs at one time? The answer is to be able to vary the entrees while putting the same vegetables on everyone's plate.

Dedication and commitment messages take care of most negative and discouragement and do not offend anyone who is new. Presenting "The Basics" with new data to support it or a new humorous anecdote will keep everyone focused and gives the new person what they need to make a quality decision to move ahead.

Having a five year curriculum helps to keep the entire team focused on continuing education and personal growth. My "Five Year Business and Leadership Development Program" is a great example.

"Feed my sheep." A good admonishment and commission to all who would be leaders... Feed the people.

Internet Notes:

The internet offers so much "fodder" for those who are hungry for knowledge. Perhaps you are stuck in the past? Your idea of "internet savvy" is getting email 3 times a week? If this is so, then you are missing out on the abundance of knowledge and wisdom that is easily accessible and for the most part free or inexpensive.

Chapter 3

FIELD DRIVEN vs.

COMPANY DRIVEN

"Work with people you like! Life's too short not to."

-- Warren Buffet, Billionaire

In a recent interview, Warren Buffet, currently ranked by Forbes magazine as the second wealthiest businessman in America, had the following observations. "How do you define the perimeter of a business? When the perimeter is well defined, it's easy to understand. When it is much larger it may be harder to understand. Coca Cola is a simple business. The perimeter is easy to define, they sell soft drinks." Many network marketing companies are hard to define. They don't know what business they are in.

When you put up a sign that says "Rock Concert" it will attract one kind of crowd. If it says "Ballet" then it will attract another kind. If you put up a sign that says "Rock Concert" when you're having a ballet, you'll have an unhappy crowd. The lesson to be learned here is to keep your business simple, look for those who can be trained, and who will commit to your business long term. Don't put up a sign that says your business is cheap, undefined, and short term;

it won't attract the kind of crowd you want!

Since 1987, I've spent most of my time consulting with companies and individual distributors in the network marketing industry. In "Raising a Giant," I dealt with the need for a strong "culture." One that's rooted in integrity and caring leadership.

The internal culture of a corporation is decidedly different than that of its entrepreneurial field force. These two seemingly contradictory cultures need to be compatible to make the best environment for success in network marketing.

Network marketers are not employees, they are independent business people. They need to be able to work on their own and in an environment of their own choosing. They work and play as they choose. They usually resent being told what to do. They eschew routine for a life of varied chores and rewards.

The typical corporate employee is not prepared for the uncertainties of being in business for themselves. They prefer a guaranteed income over the excitement of not knowing how much you will make this month. An entrepreneur is appalled at the prospect of a fixed income, the employee is appalled at the lack of security not having a fixed income brings. Imagine how many people stay in a job they hate just to get the health benefits of an insurance policy they could buy themselves.

The typical corporate line is "We can run an ad and replace a sales person any day." The typical entrepreneur in network marketing looks at the home office staff and wonders why they wouldn't rather be in the field experiencing the excitement of individual opportunity that the distributors enjoy. The general feelings of corporate employees are that the field person is overbearing and egomaniacal. The field person generally thinks the home office person doesn't take initiative and is too reliant on someone else to direct their work.

You can see the how complex the situation is when you have a "company driven" field force. Field leaders usually think of themselves as people who have "escaped" the corporate rat race. In this case, you have a dichotomy that is difficult to overcome.

When I worked in the aircraft industry as a mechanic, the engineers would send down drawings and specifications that when we tried to put it on the airplane we couldn't make it work. It looked good on paper but simply didn't work in practice. "Company driven" field forces are always discovering that the home office "think tankers" have come up with a good idea that much of the time just doesn't work in the field.

So much of network marketing is art form and is created as you go. Companies are usually good at the science and miserable at the art form. Since the business, as practiced in the field, is 60-70% art form it is difficult to manage and build a successful "company driven" business in network marketing. It has been done.

Shaklee and Mary Kay would, in my opinion, be company driven. They both however, are bent toward "direct sales" more than to network marketing. Avon would also be an example of a "company driven" company but it is more of a "direct sales company than a network marketing company.

Amway is a "field driven" company, as is NuSkin. Herbalife has blended the two mainly because Mark Hughes (now tragically deceased), the founder, was a field general and not a "home office" type. The advancement of a company depends on creative field leadership. Company driven field organizations work usually when the company leadership started in the field. (As in Mark Hughes (Herbalife), Rich DeVos and Jay VanAndel (Amway). Others have had immense difficulty defining a workable relationship with their field force. Opting for a "boss" style which rarely works with entrepreneurs.

People in the field can do things that the company could never do. For example, field organizations are made up of many small "cells." These cells are centered around small groups of personalities. The company could never track and orchestrate effective "leading edge" management of these cells. The company cannot effectively orchestrate and administer dynamic recognition programs as well as the field. (They can and should, however, provide recognition structure.) The field is more attuned to the daily moods, highs and lows of the field force and can adjust quickly to accommodate them.

The company is limited by its ability to manage from a distance. An efficient field driven business can manage and motivate locally. It is impossible for the company to drive smaller meetings and events. One of the biggest companies in the world of network marketing has tried its best to drive their business in the United States with hired field managers, and have a minuscule business to show for the millions they have invested.

Field leaders have a better sense of the mood of the organization. The field leaders are going to take a personal interest in the "individuals" in the group, where the company tends to be more detached and focused on the field organization as a "whole." Field leaders are supposed to be in the living rooms and dens of their downlines. They are busy drinking coffee and listening to challenges each individual has. They motivate and train based on individual need, whereas the company has to rely upon "cookie cutter" programs. The difference is like having a tailored made suit versus one off the rack.

When company people blow into town the attention may be diverted from where it belongs, and advice may be given which is not in concert with that being given by the local leaders. This can create a confidence crisis, and cause confusion and discomfort for everyone. Help them more by hindering them less.

The network marketing company of today must look at the advantages of "directing" the field while leaving leadership to the field. This means that the new, more effective, style of managing the growth comes from a "Company directed, Field driven approach."

The role of the company is to provide guidance, protect the integrity of the business, and do things the field cannot, and are not, most capable of doing. Print recognition is one of these things, awards and trips are another. The company should make policy decisions and guard against legal interference. The savvy company of the future will direct the overall attack from a distance. Get a good group of potential leaders, train them well, then get out of the way and let them lead.

"Field driven" businesses have been hard to come by in recent years because the talent and experience needed to provide mature leadership is not readily available. Most of the seasoned veterans are entrenched in their own companies and thus, are not available to provide leadership for new companies.

New companies may find themselves saddled with the leadership of disgruntled castoffs that either couldn't make it with other companies or didn't have the staying power to last with their previous company. Both way the company and field suffer.

This presents an interesting dilemma, because it is not in the general corporate makeup to direct field activities nor is it in the transient mentality of most available field leaders to understand long-term, stable, business development principles. How does this dilemma affect you? Very simple. Immaturity breeds mistakes, mistakes create uncertainty in the group, and uncertainty destroys the opportunity for everyone.

The solution lies in the ability for corporations to avail themselves of the best information available, and to identify early in the development process people with little or no previous network marketing experience and have them go through a leadership development program to make certain that your company is not a poor relative to some other failed endeavor. Remember, Emerson said, "The chains of habit are too light to be felt until they're too heavy to be broken."

What is needed is a new regime of untainted

leadership, mingled with those who "Have seen the light," and bonded together with a common objective to create a uniform culture that will grow and stand the test of time. Not those whose habits have doomed them to repeated mistakes and ultimate failure.

Being one who had to pay a very high price to "see the light," I am a staunch believer in the "get em young and train 'em your way" concept. Retraining is a matter of "unlearning" bad habits. It is a most difficult task.

If you had to pick someone in your acquaintance upon which you would earn ten percent of their income for the rest of your life. Who would you pick? You wouldn't pick the person with the highest grades in school. The one who looks the best or the one who speaks the best? What would you look for in them? Would you look for honesty? Integrity? Work ethic? Competence in business? While all of these characteristics are important, you would pick someone who showed initiative, who was teachable, and someone who was open-minded enough to move with the tides, but was steadfast enough not to be a flake.

In conclusion, the company of the future will be more involved with the field in decisions affecting the field. I believe that we will see the rise in "Company Directed… Field Driven" companies. The reason is that more and more legislation is impacting our world. Companies have the resources to deal with problems before they occur. (Hopefully they have the presence of mind and talent to recognize them) This requires a closer alliance with field leaders than ever before.

Also, companies tend to recognize trends earlier than

the field. They have access to all the data which no single distributor has. When they know what to look for, a savvy CEO will be able to make adjustments more quickly and avert disastrous consequences.

Watching depth charts, computer graphs of leadership development trends will give the CEO an in depth minute to minute tracking system that can be valuable to field leaders. Understanding the lag time between recruiting and sales helps a great deal. And understanding what drives recruiting is effort... and in today's computer driven world there is no reason not to have the data to analyze to determine when the effort is diminished.

Experience:

Most successful distributors spend the first 5 years of their networking life building in Phase I of the business... sponsor everyone who can fog a mirror. No time is given to the understanding of other phases of leadership development. They have 1 year of experience repeated 5 times. However, companies will inevitably allow these same people to advise them on "compensation plan enhancements" and other leadership changes they know little or nothing about.

The inmates are running the asylum.

Internet Notes:

eMarketing solutions can magnify the appeal of network marketing. Stay at home moms, new retirees, and young entrepreneurs want to live life in "their" idea of freedom. Not in an office or warehouse with a nine to five job. Study how emarketing can help you.

Chapter 4

THE FIVE KEYS TO RETENTION

"Give up small beliefs, Give up pretense, Give up comfortable traditions."
-- Dr. Leo Buscaglia

The most significant thing that stands out to those of us who have been in the industry for very long is how easily the masses give up. I am asked quite often... what does the average person do in network marketing? My answer usually surprises them when I tell them that the "average person" quits.

So what else is new? The average person has been taught to quit. They have been told not to beat a dead horse, to give up quickly and move on to the next deal only to quit there too. The average person "wants to succeed," but they "expect to fail." No wonder retention rates in the industry are so low. Much of our time is spent dealing with socially and emotionally challenged misfits!

Retention is the biggest problem most network

36

marketing companies face. In "Raising a Giant," I covered the "Funnel and the Bucket" concept. The "Funnel" puts them in; the "Bucket" keeps them in. To get people to ultimately build a downline, you must have programs to keep them around and move them along at a pace acceptable to both of you.

The first order of business is to make sure we know how to deal with life's three biggest killers; fear, lethargy and indifference! A man was asked by a reporter how he felt about the prevalence of ignorance and apathy, he said, "I don't know and I don't care."

Fear takes on all sorts of characteristics: Fear of failure, fear of success, fear of being left out, fear of being found out, fear of speaking to others, fear of being taken advantage of, fear of not being rewarded properly and so on.

Fear is based for the most part in lack of self-esteem or self-confidence. It is true that your "self-worth" will determine your "net worth." These issues must be dealt with before the actual process of building a great organization will take place. Let me also advise that this is a never ending battle. Vigilance in the battle against public enemy number one is demanded!

There are five keys to defeating the enemy of fear and indifference. They are Inspiration, Information, Activation, Recognition, and Confirmation. These can be best depicted as a cycle. They revolve around one another and are not isolated activities.

INSPIRATION - Encouraging The Mass

So much has been said about inspiration that it seems almost ludicrous to take up time here to explore it. However, I find that in visiting with most of the new network marketing leaders that many do not understand that effort is preceded by inspiration.

My upline always focused teaching people to dream again. Children don't have to be taught to dream. Somewhere in adulthood we forget how. The truth is that everyone has a dream. Getting people to build relies entirely on the connection between the business and their dream.

We are all inspired by the words to the hit song, "The Impossible Dream" whose lyrics admonish us to "Follow the dream, no matter how hopeless, no matter how far," to "fight for the right without question or pause, to be willing to march into hell for a heavenly cause." Who can forget Whitney Houston's, "One Moment in Time" that challenged us with the inspiring words, "When all of my dreams are a heartbeat away, and the answer is all up to me."

How can any alert leader NOT spend much of their focus on inspiring themes, events, and materials? Wall Street and Madison Avenue use inspirational themes to sell billions of dollars of goods and services to us. Most of the growth in the stock market can be attributed to "investor inspiration."

MCI's "Friends and Family" program is designed to touch our heart-strings. A new Volvo commercial shows an adorable child sitting in the back seat of a car in a car seat, and closes with, "At Volvo we don't think any child should be seated in the front seat of any car." An obviously emotionally charged commercial appeal designed to sell their cars.

Nike pays famous athletes like Michael Jordan and Tiger Woods millions to be role models for kids so that they will buy Nike products. People are inspired to act, (This means spend and work) by role models. Yet, very few of the new network marketing companies I advise or evaluate focus on the emotional side of the business. It is easier to focus on selling the benefits of their latest and greatest product than it is to "reach out and touch someone." It's no wonder that the desertion rate is so high. Remember the admonishment, "People don't care how much you know, until they know how much you care."

People respond to themes, awards programs, buttons that proclaim outrageous goals, banners, funny or touching songs, cheers and cheerleaders. Even the late great Pete Rozelle, the commissioner of the National Football League, who invented the Super Bowl couldn't sell out the first two events. It wasn't until the third year that the Super Bowl sold out! Now you can't touch a ticket for an end zone seat for less than five hundred dollars!

I recently met a man named Art Berg. Art is a quadriplegic, but his life is an inspiration to all who meet him. He is a competitor, author, and motivational speaker, His own story is an inspiration to all who meet him.

The late Wilma Rudolph had polio as a child and yet became an Olympic champion! We are capable of incredible things when properly inspired. Take time to award plaques, trophies, trips, dinners, and massive applause. Don't just "have" a recognition program, but become "obsessed" with it!

INFORMATION - *Focusing the Collective Mind of the Mass*

The second key to retention is information. Remember Mary Kay Ash's admonishment that "Inspiration without information creates frustration." However, the reverse is true as well; information without inspiration will produce absolutely nothing! Every event should be filled with both inspiration and information. Remember the Madison Avenue approach and don't forget the pizzazz! Keep the factual messages simple and to the point but present them with panache!

Information can be divided into three categories. One is product information. Too few people in network marketing actually know enough about the benefits of their product lines. Not just the ingredients, but what the products really do. How do they compare with the competition? Most people are content with just saying, "Our products are the best" without giving any real concrete reasons why.

Third party material from newspapers, magazines, the internet and outside experts. Testimonies from those who have used the products and liked them. Price comparisons may be useful as is research data and double blind study results.

The second information area deals with business building techniques. This includes a solid well-defined getting started program. Things as basic as making prospect lists, while important, are incomplete. A prospect list that includes vital "inside information" about the prospects on the list would be much more helpful. What kind of people are we looking for? How are they related to the new distributor? What are their present occupations? Do they have any previous network marketing experience? Are they presently working with another network marketing company?

As a side issue to this question, let me remind you that when a new member talks to someone from another company they are at risk themselves to be "reversed." Reversing is when your member gets turned on to the other guy's deal and decides to leave you to go to the other side. This can also happen when new people follow-up leads from newspaper and magazine ads.

New members need some counseling on such things as how much and what kind of products should they buy to get started. Are there any discounts or bonus incentives they need to know about? When is the next event? How about training opportunities? Who's Who in their upline and how can they get in touch with them? These are vital areas which when covered thoroughly will increase retention of new members several percentage points. It is a proven fact that people who get "plugged in" to their upline early in the game are more likely to stay in the business.

The third area is in the details. What kind of paperwork is there? How to fill out forms, order products, advance up the bonus scale? What do I need to do to qualify for trips, are there advanced training programs and increased leadership responsibilities? What is expected of me and what can I expect in the way of help from my sponsor, the company, and my upline leadership? Provide them a business plan early and be sure that it is a complete one.

The confused mind says no. So be clear about your instructions. Keep it simple but dynamic. Don't leave anything to the imagination. The new distributor should not be confused with complex formulas, marketing plan data which will not apply to them for a while, or building depth concepts. Too many people today are trying to dazzle new distributors with their knowledge of complicated bonus plans and theories.

Provide every new prospect with a uniform "Literature Pack" that includes testimonial CDs and DVDs on both the business opportunity AND the product effectiveness. Have a standardized "Get Started" program. Keep it simple, say if often, and make it burn!

ACTIVATION - Moving the Mass

Activation is the key to early success and thus a retention rate that exceeds the norm. Activation, which has at its roots the key word "activity", is not simply activity, but an entire process of moving a massive group of people toward a commonly held goal. Focusing the "Collective mind of the mass" on effort is essential. Individually, everyone can make a difference, but collectively, you can change the world.

The true leader is obsessed with group growth and understands the need for accountability programs. This is a widely misunderstood and ignored process. To some, accountability means having a boss or someone looking over your shoulder telling you what to do. Sometimes a negative connotation is associated with accountability.

Sam Walton, the deceased founder of Wal-Mart said in his book, "Made in America" that a good manager will "give someone a job to do, trust them to do it, then check on them and confirm that they did it." This is also true with network marketing. Sam's contention was that everyone liked to be recognized for doing a good job and that by checking to confirm that it was done you were in fact reaffirming the person's capability and building their self-esteem. He contended that the next job assigned would be done better when the person realized he/she was going to be checked on to see how well they did.

This is part of the art form of the business and requires tactfulness and a good deal of finesse to make a positive experience. Since it is true that ours is a "volunteer army," then we cannot in effect "fire" someone for messing up or failing to do what we expected or what they said they were going to do. We can however, provide a venue and process by which the checking up procedure is a reminder that someone upline cares about your progress and therefore your ultimate success. This is the difference in the "boss attitude" versus "the caring leader" attitude.

Activation is the act of taking full responsibility for moving the entire organization to action. Once I printed up twenty million dollars in "Crisp Cash" which was nothing more than fifty and one hundred dollar bills with my picture on them. I took care to have the bills printed on good paper, in money green ink, and cut to perfect size to give the impression of real money. I then had the money banded in bands of ten thousand dollars and placed into real Brinks money bags with the $1,000,000 printed on the outside.

I had a meeting in a central location with my top four hundred leaders. I gave them a comprehensive "plan of action." I had my top fifteen to twenty leaders (those that represented the rest) come up to the stage where this massive pile of twenty million dollars was stacked. I gave each a bag of one million dollars and a set of printed rules for doling it out. I gave each leader there a pack of 1000 flyers explaining the program and how the cash could be earned and used, and we were off and running.

The leaders had each contributed to the prize fund, an amount commensurate with the size of their organizations and income, to pay for prizes to be sold at "auction" at our next major event. Needless to say the sponsoring took off and sales of products soared. Everyone got excited! People who had done nothing got involved, new pin levels were reached and we had a record breaking quarter!

I personally invested heavily in awards and gifts for my top people putting them on a different level with their groups and out of the competition with their downlines, and kept the excitement going throughout the campaign.

The leader must be focused on group activity and is responsible to lead the mass toward monthly, quarterly and annual achievement levels.

When weekly meetings stall out, the leader must create a crisis situation. Once or twice a year I would get a meeting room with twice as many chairs as I expected I would need. I roped off the back half of the room before the meeting.

At the close of the meeting I asked all those interested in doubling the size of their business to stay. I asked the audience to finish this sentence..... "A chain is only as strong as its weakest _____" (Link) then asked,

"How many weak links do we have here tonight?" The answer of course is "None."

I went back and placed two of my business cards on each of two empty chairs in the back, told them that I would like each of them to do the same. These would represent the places the new prospects at next week's meeting would sit.

I would collect the cards in order and replace them before the meeting next week. We would all be held accountable for doing our part in doubling the business in one week! Everyone would know who the weak links were!

This approach won't work every week but it will work when things inevitably stall out.

Forming baseball, football, or basketball teams and leagues with points given and competitions held will create esprit de corps and get things moving when they are slow.

RECOGNITION - Rewarding the Mass

Recognition builds volume, volume builds checks, and checks create new life-style patterns which lead eventually to a greater desire level, which will then create a new level of activity and aspiration.

Leaders spend too little time studying what has and can be done regarding recognition! Art Williams, the controversial founder of the A.L. Williams (Now Primerica) gave away cheap tee shirts with slogans on them to anyone who did almost anything at an event that was special.

A loud cheer got you a tee shirt; a bright necktie got you a tee shirt; a pretty smile, enthusiastic handshake got you a tee shirt; bring a new member you get a tee shirt. He gave away tee shirts to everyone who did anything! His slogan was "At our company we believe in recognition, lots of it, we give trophies the size of men and plaques the size of doors." The results speak for themselves!

So if it has been proven to work so well why doesn't everyone do it? Why do most of the network marketing companies and organization leaders miss so badly on this vital issue? Why is it that Mary Kay, Amway, and Tupperware seem to be the only companies who really hit the mark when it comes to inspiration and recognition? They don't hide what they do. They do it out in the open for everyone to see and duplicate. Sure other companies make an attempt, but most fall short of a first class effort. Amway's first yacht was less than 100 feet. Their current one is nearly 200 feet long and they have several!

I've heard it one too many times, "We don't want to be like Amway." Do you hear opera singers say they don't want to sing like Pavarotti? Or race car drivers who don't want to drive like Al Unser or A.J. Foyt? What would you think of a basketball player who didn't want to do the things Michael Jordan did or Kobe Bryant and Lebron James do now? You'd think they were crazy right?

Not that everyone should duplicate everything that Amway, Shaklee or Mary Kay does, but we should at least study their successes and duplicate the good things. They don't have a franchise on great recognition programs... someone will give away jets, villas in the South of France or Italy... Rolls Royces and Bentleys will be awarded... the bar will be raised.

So why do most network marketing pros miss the boat so badly? The answer is not as important as the acknowledgment that you are weak in this area. What interests me the most is the opportunities that this massive failure offers... I believe that new companies who are funded well enough to put into place award programs and inspire their people to action will dominate the future.

We will explore recognition and its effects throughout this book. Recognition is a part of every productive thing a leader does in network marketing. It may be true throughout the whole of life's experiences that those who recognize others are the ones who enjoy the greatest rewards in this life.

Recognition systems begin with a "Getting Started" award. We used a monthly event called "Thousand Dollar Club" to get our new people to focus on their first significant goal. We would have a dinner on the first Friday night of every month (Date night). No formalities, we chose an inexpensive but nice restaurant.

Sometimes we would have a cook- out at my house or beach party, or picnic. It was a big deal and it got everyone involved. If you brought a new qualifier, you could pick up the tab as a reward. (The tab was usually much less than the profit you made on their volume.) You introduced your new member, who told the group something about themselves. It gave them a sense of belonging and let all of us get better acquainted.

Recognition must be withheld from those who don't qualify. Fear of loss as well as opportunity for gain must be emphasized! You can't have an "in" group if you don't have an "out" group. The key to making this a positive rather than a negative is to let everyone know that they are welcome to the "in" group anytime they meet the standard. You also can't have an "in" group unless you do something that distinguishes them from the rest. Those qualified get to attend a banquet, special training retreat, or working vacation with the group.

Special pins and awards that are a part of a systematic growth plan are vital. You'd be surprised how much mileage you can get out of a $2.00 lapel pin and a few seconds of praise on stage at the monthly event and when coupled with your emarketing solutions you will have them eating out of your hands soon.

Progressive Departures

My upline kept the goals in front of us at all times. Rarely did we have an event that we did not do a "progressive departure." A progressive departure is just what the name implies. At an event you make an announcement that those who are qualified at a certain level will have an advanced training opportunity at the conclusion of the meeting. You ask those who are not qualified to leave and speak to those who stay.

During these special times you can do some really inspiring dreams sessions, go over special events coming up and talk about leadership goals. You then progressively dismiss achievement levels until you are down to a handful. Then, have something special planned to do with these few afterward. This is a powerful tool. Use it wisely.

CONFIRMATION - *Holding the Mass Accountable*

Completing the cycle of retention improvement is the concept of Confirmation. This is the broadest view of the entire success cycle in the process. The leader must use his/her vision to see the entire operation.

When the United States decides to go to war, the enlisted man simply says, "Give me a gun and tell me who to shoot." The line officers see the daily activities required to carry out the operation. The senior officers make operational policy and oversee distribution of supplies and dissemination of needed data and information.

The commanding officers however, see the entire picture. How many tanks, guns, ammunition will be required? What are the food needs, how much flour, vegetables, eggs, corn, bread, milk, butter and so on... They calculate the necessary transportation needs, fighter planes, helicopters, medical personnel and supplies. Likewise, the true network marketing leader calculates the needs of the entire organization.

Confirmation means leaving nothing to chance. How successful would an Army General be if he didn't think of all the details of fighting a war? How successful will you be when you or someone in your upline doesn't see the big picture?

Alexander the Great, who conquered the known world at the age of twenty-six, fed his soldiers on grain purchased from Egypt, not those grown in his native Greece, because the nutrients in the Egyptian grain would allow his soldiers to have the energy to march further and fight with passion. He studied the art of war and was aware of all the details.

Confirmation means looking at the four other elements: Inspiration, Information, Activation, and Recognition to see if they are being done and done well! The leader's job is not for wimps or weenies. This is an adult job with massive consequences.

In summary, the importance of products cannot be down played, but it is business builders, those who recruit and train others, that make the industry prosperous. Once the issue of high quality products, competitively priced has been established, the best thing you can do is focus on the building techniques. Working with people is what it is all about. People sell products, products don't sell people.

Internet Notes:

eMarketing means email marketing coupled with online training systems and in depth tracking systems. Today data collection and deciphering should be every person's ardent desire and number one job. Knowing what to do with the data is the key ingredient... but knowing what to do without a current well programmed database software system is ludicrous.

Chapter 5

DEBUNKING THE MYTH

"Power establishes itself through service, and perishes through abuse." -- Victor Duruy

Nothing is more devastating than having someone you trust give you erroneous information... especially if you are investing significant amounts of time and money relying upon the accuracy of the information. Probably more negative is derived from this than all of the other complaints about network marketing combined.

Who wants to lose credibility with friends and business associates because the information you gave them came from a "reliable" source which turned out to be not so reliable?

It is for this reason that people who have been burned many times are reluctant to go back to friends and family (their warm market) to share their current opportunity. Instead, we have seen a proliferation of "cold market," "mail order" programs. I guess the reasoning is "It is better to deceive a stranger than to deceive a friend." Wouldn't the best advice seem to be that no reward is worth the deception of innocent people?

We need to clean up some misconceptions and enlist our fellow network marketing professionals, regardless of their company affiliations, to help in the effort.

While there are many such myths and misconceptions, I am going to deal with only the most prevalent and destructive here.

"Get Rich Quick"

How can anyone with half a brain buy into this crock of baloney?   Since we're on the subject, why is it that in my home state of California, when the state lottery exceeds fifty million dollars, you have to stand in line to get a ticket? The month previous I didn't stand in line and the lottery was a measly thirty odd million! What's the matter? Didn't these people need the thirty mil? I guess what P.T. Barnum said is true, there is "A fool born every minute." Having said that doesn't excuse those of us who exercise the gray matter a little bit from approaching the opportunity with some degree of restraint and reason.

Look, the workaday world offers a lousy deal. Forty years of working for subsistence wages should be enough to cause everyone to seek out a network marketing company to be involved in. The real deal is a good deal. Even if it took ten years to build financial independence through a solid network marketing company, the result would be exceedingly better than the typical nine to five existence of a job.

Why do we have to make the opportunity sound like a used car salesman trying to pawn a lemon off on our grandmother? My fax machine goes off every night with some of the wildest, way out, heal you in minute schemes I've ever heard of, and these people are serious! The problem seems to emanate from those who haven't been able to build a legitimate downline by good old fashion hard work, so they seek out the weakest and most naive to perpetrate their latest and greatest fraud.

It also emanates from a theory that network marketing companies as a whole have a limited life expectancy. It propounds the theory that you must "catch the wave" or "ride the momentum." Then, when this deal runs its course you can go on to the next deal. The problem with this is that it has turned the network marketing industry into a lottery proposition instead of a legitimate method for getting goods and services into the hands of consumers.

"Bended Knee Theory"

The "Bended Knee Theory" contends that there is a "right time" to enter a network marketing company, which then in turn would imply that there is a "wrong time" to enter one. The truth is if you're concerned about timing; find a more established company where the timing is always right!

It is with the fragile start-ups that timing becomes an issue. Mainly because they likely won't be around for long (90% failure rate), so you have to get in early because those who get in late are in a world of hurt!

My first experience in network marketing was with a company that was sixteen years old. Everyone told me nobody would be interested in the deal, that it had reached "saturation." In the next four years, I still found two hundred thousand believers! Those who thought the deal had reached its full potential found themselves eating crow.

Today, that same company (At the time a two hundred million dollar a year company) does over six billion dollars of sales worldwide! I guess it hadn't peaked yet.

"The Saturation Myth"

No company has been so good that they have been able to reach this mystical status. There are many reasons for this. One is that competition has kept any one company from totally dominating the marketplace. In the early days, Shaklee and Amway pretty much had it to themselves. Today, there are over two thousand network marketing companies, of which two hundred or so are good solid stable opportunities. More Fortune 500 companies have entered the arena and you can bet that there will be mega-companies who see the network marketing industry as a dynamic way to sell their products and services as well.

Companies such as NuSkin and Herbalife have stood the test of time and have hundreds of millions in sales annually. There are other fine opportunities that are well funded and managed that present great opportunities. The "Saturation" and "Bended Knee" theorists are full of hot air.

The truth is that companies and organizations go through cycles. While one country or group may be slowing down or static, others are blooming and growing! Things change, people change, leadership regimes come and go, people who were working fourteen hour days cut back, take vacations, move to the mountains or sea. All of these elements determine the present state of growth in any business.

It is an unfair or misleading observation to say that any company has "topped out." Sure, some companies grow only to the capacity of the leadership or ownership to manage and motivate, but in time, even these evolve into new and hopefully better habit patterns and produce a new growth curve.

"Get in Early Myth"

Those who propound this theory are distorting the truth of network marketing and discounting some very solid business advice.

First, more established companies tend to have systems in place which assure a steady and reliable stream of quality products and seasoned management.

Second, information and data systems are debugged and working properly. Start-ups are using their new distributors as Ginny pigs… experimenting with pay plans and products day by day. There is no truth at all in the belief that "Only those who get in early will make the big money." The company I started with was a sixteen year old company that everyone said was over the hill.

I believe one should always look for opportunity, but not at the cost of security and common sense. Look, network marketing is hard enough without having to drag the home office, or your upline, around with you every day!

In short the mythological Tooth Fairy, Santa Claus, Brinks Truck Wreck, Relative Dying and leaving you Money and so on is about as likely to happen as the Duracell Bunny switching to Rayovac.

It's time to appreciate the beauty in investing yourself

in a great opportunity with a knowledgeable upline and efficient and well managed company. Short cuts never are! In its real and unadulterated form, network marketing is a deal nearly too good to be true!

Quit painting mustaches on the Mona Lisa.

Internet Notes:

Early adapters are people who adapt to new technologies long before others discover them. The internet is just beginning… it has taken 20 years for adults around the world to lose their fear of the computer. High speed, broadband connections now cover most of the globe… an email doesn't need permission or a passport to cross borders and do business. If you're not "there" yet… get there quickly… find a teacher / mentor to show you how to hookup to the many social networks that exist… facebook, myspace, linkedin, plaxo, and twitter.com.

Chapter 6

THE ONION EFFECT

"Buy a simple business that is so simple an idiot can run it because eventually one will." -- Warren Buffet

When I first entered the network marketing industry my sponsor told me that this would be the easiest thing I ever did. Boy was he way out in left field (Probably lied about being a professional baseball pitcher too). I have never done anything more difficult than network marketing. It is the most exasperating, aggravating, frustrating business I've ever tried my hand at. However, once I got the hang of it, it was quite intoxicating, stimulating, and certainly rewarding.

As I built, I began to discover things about myself I didn't know. I found my skills with people, while better developed than most, were lacking. I realized that there was much to learn. Like most of you I had to try it "My Way" at first. Reinventing the wheel is not exactly a wise use of time. My sixth month bonus check was a measly $3.63! Not quite an amount worthy of a major press release.

The larger my group got the more I discovered I didn't know. It was quite a revelation. It amazes me when I read about people who have been in network marketing for two or three years who have set themselves up as network marketing "Professionals." My mentor once brought a Bible on stage during a leadership meeting and reminded us that even the best teacher who ever lived took three years to teach his frontline (Disciples) how to carry on in his absence. He pointed out to us that since he was somewhat less capable than the Man from Galilee, we were probably in for a longer training period. Great wisdom don't you think?

The network marketing business is much like an onion. Peeling away one layer reveals another and so on until you get through to the core. Beginning leadership skills are unlike advanced techniques. Do you think we needed to send the same number of troops to Grenada as we did to Iraq? No. Overkill you say? True. Then you should know that the dynamics of growth are not the same as the dynamics of shrinkage. And yet everyone will have to endure a downward turn in their business eventually. It's the way things work.

I was totally unprepared for the modest downturn my business took. The preceding five years we enjoyed nothing but unrestricted growth. I thought it would never end! But end it did! And when my downline began to see their checks go down, their volume fall, the attendance at meetings decline, I didn't have a clue what to do.

I longed for someone with previous experience in turning it around. But having unwisely turned my back on my source of wisdom, I found myself grasping at straws and making it up as I went. Not a good idea. I had cut myself off from the most important training I could ever get. How do I keep my group "in" when they are not going forward? How do I explain to my leaders that we are "just experiencing a slight market adjustment?" Who could I turn to, to reinforce to my leaders that I'm still a good guy with their best interests in mind?

The answer was no one. Not important you say? Over- night-sensations, pie-in-the-sky-by-and-by nitwits, and egocentric morons, will never recognize that the dynamics of leadership changes as groups get larger. Leadership of thousands and even hundreds of thousands is quite different than that of leading a few hundred. In the chapter titled, "Five Keys to Retention" we discussed the concept of "Activation and Confirmation."

Who do you turn to when no one in your company or upline have ever been there before? New ground is being broken and no one knows if they are going to dig up Dracula with an opportunity meeting suit on and a fax on demand prospect list. What happens to these giant mail-order downlines when the next person with wet tongue, a role of stamps, a hot new recruiting tape, and a list of names bought from a guy named Swiftly, in the back alley, contacts your downline with the latest and greatest deal?

Nurturing skills… motivational skills… counseling skills… dream building skills… business development skills. Things as innocent as listening skills… stage skills… person to person interaction skills.

The bigger you get, the more the demands on you become. If you abdicate your responsibility, then you and your group will suffer. That dream of retiring in the mountains or by the sea with a six figure income will become another fantasy and you will be back on the job before you know it.

The good book says "He that walketh with the wise, grows wise," a good admonition. So often I see the blind leading the blind. The answers are not always simple, because the root of the problems may be complex. You can't solve every problem by telling the group to go sponsor someone else.

I recently heard someone who is suppose to be a leading guru to the network marketing elite instruct one of his leaders to "Stop calling your downline and spend all of your time sponsoring new people." I couldn't believe my ears. No wonder this person's company has been stagnant for years!

Network marketing is not a case of "Throwing enough on the wall." It is a business that relies upon learnable, teachable skills. What chance would someone like me have had with an upline who held me by the hand for two weeks and then left me to fend for myself? The answer is none.

I guess there are some who think that the Master Teacher was just not as good as they are, after all, they can accomplish in two weeks what the good Lord took three years to do. Wake up! Pay attention! This is not Fantasy Island where all you gotta do is meet someone with a midget and a white suit and all your dreams will become reality.

I divide the learning curve "onion" into five segments.

1. Basic Training

2. Intermediate Training

3. Advanced Training

4. Leadership Development I

5. Leadership Development II

BASIC TRAINING

Basic Training is your "How to Get Started" program. This needs to be as simple as possible. Don't let this get too complicated. As a part of this training, you want to give the new member an easy to comprehend plan for initiating action as well as an overview of the road ahead. Today's new distributor is smarter and wiser than in times past. I think most people are more likely to stay in the deal when they know there is a rock solid game plan in place for future training.

Basic Training should be able to be covered in two hours or less. It obviously should include product knowledge as well as business building advice. As a part of the basic training program, it is vital to introduce new members to their upline. Several generations of upline phone numbers should be available.

Anyone who earns money on what you do should be willing to tell you how to get in touch with them. My entire two hundred thousand person downline had my phone number and knew that I was available to encourage and counsel them.

If I were President of the United States, I would have a phone number that was published in every newspaper in America and would set aside a few hours every week to take and return phone calls. You may not be able to talk personally with everyone, but you must give them the impression that you are trying.

As an added note to communications here, a major

network marketing magazine recently ran an article about a large distributor for an industry giant. The magazine quoted the distributor, "Everyday we turn the telephones off at 6 PM so we can have time with our family." Now the implication here is suppose to be that this is a good thing to do if you love your family. (Hard to argue with that.) However, ninety percent of the people in network marketing are part-timers; they have jobs and businesses to run other than their network marketing business.

What this couple was saying was, "When you need us, and have the time to talk to us (After 6 PM), we are going to turn our phones off and turn our backs on your family to take care of ours." Selfish don't you think? And destructive!

Imagine everyone in a large organization who did what this couple did. No work after 6 PM! INCREDIBLE! New people must have a sense of "connectedness" to the power players upline. The couple in the article would have been far better served to have said that two or three nights a week are set aside for family time. Even if they did in fact turn the phones off, I would never ever have told anyone about it!

In your basic training, you want to indoctrinate, inform and inspire, talk about your culture and vision. This is not the time to go overboard on anything except an abiding commitment to the opportunity that your company offers. The outline is simple "People, Products, and Programs."

INTERMEDIATE TRAINING-INTERNSHIP

Intermediate Training is where we get into the actual building process. Until now, all we have concentrated on is familiarization with products, bonus plan details and prospect lists. The initial thirty day period, or until someone actually has a few people sponsored in their downline, there isn't any reason to go into detailed discussions of business building.

Now the new distributor is ready for some real meat. We begin with the process of teaching the new distributor how to get someone else started. (This may seem elementary but chances are they weren't paying much attention when you got them started.)

You don't want to turn the existing group over to a neophyte to handle, but you do want them to get some experience, so you ask them to sponsor and work with some new people. The small downline groups that you have been working with, you continue to work with personally. This is your security. In hospitals, usually interns don't "do" the surgery they "assist." The same is true in this instance; the person who is ready to advance to this training level needs to understand the internship program.

In this training we do not want to exhaust the supply of information available. We want to explain the "whys and wherefores" of "The System." We want to introduce them to new levels of commitment and to propose attainment of higher levels of achievement and to lock them into more training!

Remember to deal with the issues that confront the average American two income family. How do you handle baby-sitter problems? Why should both husband and wife attend functions? Setting the right example for their new downline. Take charge of the income and expenses of building their business. It is vital to point out the many ways the business can be negatively affected by poor money management. Review goals and plan how to reach the next level of success in your business.

ADVANCED TRAINING

Advanced training takes place in a more controlled environment. Usually at some resort or isolated retreat. The importance of this beyond the actual activity itself is that it creates a goal for those who are moving up to attain. How do I qualify for the more advanced training? Answer? Move to the next level. These events are geared to deepen the commitment and broaden the sense of responsibility for those wanting to be "full-time" in the business. These are "Challenge" events. The idea is to shake up the status quo.

Now we can get really serious. Hard hitting allowed. This is not for wimps, weenies or the weak of spirit. This is a training that challenges everyone to reach inside and go beyond past performance levels. Look, if no one asks more of us then who will find the necessity to do more? There is no cure for running away. This is a great time for sharing and relating.

Here we are going to get into working depth properly. We will show how to drive each leg deep and how to explode the business once the leg has a hundred to two hundred people in the downline and is at least ten levels deep in the deepest leg. (Usually you can take a leg doing five to ten thousand of volume and get it to two hundred to five hundred thousand in ninety to one hundred and twenty days!) In my own advanced leadership seminars I explain in detail how to do this.

LEADERSHIP I

Leadership I is about assessing weaknesses and strengths, isolating your own top leadership and learning to move masses of people toward a common objective. There is nothing more frustrating than having to rebuild a leg. My upline advised me to "Build it once." He meant that I should stay in a leg until there was more than enough evidence that someone else cared more about that legs success than I did.

He also advised that I should back that person up with someone who cared more than they did. He said that this would give me security for my own future income and pretty much assure me that I was through working in that leg as a matter of the building process.

Let me point out however, that the hard work may be just beginning, that is to sustain growth during the leadership transfer. Strangely enough, the network marketing world has wrought some diverse opinions about when and how to "pullout" of a leg. In the Leadership I course, we discuss when and how to "back out" of a leg.

LEADERSHIP II

Leadership II is a more advanced version of Leadership I. Usually, leaders have misunderstood how to handle the egos and skills of their downline leaders, and problems have arisen that they have difficulty handling. Leadership II revisits the key elements in handling problem areas in the business. By the time someone gets to this training, they should have been in the business two years or longer and should have a downline of several thousand.

At this point, we have come full circle. We started with personal growth and continued at each level to challenge the emerging leaders to expand their horizons and skills. Now conflict is rising, egos are emerging, and we are challenged to deal with new issues.

Much of this book will be misunderstood until you have gone through the problems. Until I had a leg of over seven thousand disappear, I couldn't believe that it could happen. How fragile is the business? How resilient? Leadership II is all about managing a business doing millions of dollars of sales volume and yielding millions of dollars of income to several people. Doesn't it surprise anyone that so few take the responsibility of these incomes / families seriously?

These are giant businesses with much at stake everyday! It takes a giant to run a giant business. One of the largest companies in our industry had a very successful business flourishing right here in Southern California. As it grew, so did the income of some very talented people. Their incomes grew so much that they were able to quit their jobs, go full time, and move away. They moved out of the area where they had built the income and gave the appearance of having "retired to a life of leisure."

The problem was those they left "In charge" also moved away. What do you expect? People duplicate their upline. Three years later, the business in the area is in a shambles. Fragmented and torn apart by wolves. No one to guard the hen house... No one to shelter the newborns or give hope to the hopeless.

Now the upline is faced with rebuilding. What should they have done? Aren't we suppose to be able to retire, move to our dream home, fish, play golf, write books or play with our children? The answer is of course, but there is an appropriate time and way to achieve the desired result.

The challenge was that there wasn't really a new base of leadership established before the key people moved. The transfer of power and influence needs to take place gradually. New leaders need to be phased in over the span of years. There needs to be a sense of absolute uselessness to your participation. Even then, my suggestion would have been to move into a "vacation retreat" keeping my home and offices in place in the core area where I built my business. The "group" should have felt nothing amiss in the passing of the baton to someone else.

There you have it… The Onion Effect. There are many sub-layers to this onion. Not knowing how to peal it will make even the toughest cry. I promise you, short cuts don't work. To grow wise, walk with the wise, eat with the wise, cry with the wise, live wisely.

Be silent and listen to the harmonies of life. Sometimes the blind see, the deaf hear, and the lame walk again. Miracles occur every day, but no miracle is as great as the miracle of the birth of a leader. This is a long journey, made up of many years, involving many people and incidents good and bad, celebrate it and embrace it. This may be your destiny and it just might lead you to your finest hour.

SUMMARY

Learning to develop a great network marketing business takes time. Young leaders need older mentors. Maturity and seasoning takes time. Growing in wisdom and understanding the exercise of power takes time. You can't bake a cake in a hurry. All the ingredients must be made available and used.

Chapter 7

PROTOCOLS

"Success comes to those who can join hands and cooperatively move in the direction of achieving common goals." -- Napoleon Hill

There is a right way and a wrong way to do everything. And no, the end does not justify the means! Many of the mistakes that cost new network marketing companies are subtle. While everyone is busy with the products, information systems, bonus checks, sales volume and sponsoring, no one is paying any attention to the fact that the little things are killing you.

Governments hold official functions, they host heads of state and have established a protocol for seating, who comes into the room first, how is the table set? What is on the menu? Network marketing companies rarely realize that there is a protocol that must be adhered to as well.

I once represented a company whose owner was uncontrollable. This guy was his own worst enemy. Talk about the three stooges, this guy was Larry, Moe and Curly all by himself. At the first major function we did, he invited one of the larger distributors to go to dinner and bring along some of his own leaders. What is wrong with that you say? Everything! One, he made a display of having the limo pick him and those he was treating, in front of the hotel where the whole group was staying. Hundreds of deserving distributors watched in horror as "The Prez" took his "pets" out to eat.

It was a huge deal! Protocol was violated big time! Those he offended never forgave him. What he meant as an innocent gesture turned out to be devastating! Every day, owners, upline leaders, and key home office employees are subject to scrutiny. The smallest things can become blown out of proportion and literally create a situation that some can never recover from and why? So that an owner or upline leader can massage their ego and say, "It's my life and my business and I'll do whatever I want?"

I think most of the owners and key leaders in the industry are not as calloused and cold as to want the organizations they worked hard to build to disappear, because of some slight, which with forethought, could have been avoided. Instead, I believe consideration needs to be given to the big picture where everyone's needs can be met and needless hurt feelings can be avoided.

I believe that avoiding hurt feelings is a must. The absolute power that can be gained by an organization that goes to great lengths to see to it that everyone is treated fairly. That those who deserve attention and recognition get it without regard to station in life.

The network marketing industry is an "Aristocracy of achievement." A "meritocracy" my upline called it! Where everyone can be King or Queen! There should be no dark rooms to hide the politics or special interest groups. Double dealing and favoritism has no place in a healthy network marketing company. The network marketing company I want to associate with does things that uplift and build the individuals self-esteem and confidence.

Rich DeVos, the cofounder and President of Amway, could walk through a room of thousands and have a way of making the most insignificant person in the room feel important. I was amazed at his ability to look at everyone at once. I watched little old ladies hug him and he would look at them as if the business of a lifetime relied on whether they liked him or not. I crave that talent don't you? It says simply, "Make me feel important to you today!"

Offend the fewest, inspire the most! This should be our motto daily. Here are some of the most common offences and the solutions to dealing with them.

1. Don't do anything for one you wouldn't do for everyone. Shake hands and smile like a politician running for office. Be up anytime you're in sight of the group or anyone in the group. Never let the group see you down, angry or negative!

2. When you are with the group be with them. Don't isolate yourself, like some God who danes to come down from Olympus to feed with the fallen. At banquets get up, grab a pot of coffee and pour, pour, pour. I was dining at the famous Simpson's on the Strand restaurant in London once. All the servers and waiters had on white tunics with differing hash marks and decorations that I found out the hard way indicated the special nature of their service. I turned to one of them and asked for coffee. He looked at me with disgust and said, "Sir I carve, I do not pour." (As he pointed to the hash marks on his sleeve) Don't be like him! Pour, pour, and pour some more. I never eat at a banquet. I circulate, talk, take pictures, ask if all is right with the service, grab waiters for service and generally take care of the group.

3. Never insult someone or chew out a leader in front of the group. It hurts you and the person you are upbraiding. If I have a problem, I take the person aside and in private, give them grief like they have never had grief before. Never take a person's dignity. Never!

Spouses who are not involved in the business should not attend functions, unless they are going to sit in the function and participate like everyone else. Leave little children at home with a baby-sitter. Meetings and events are not the place for children, especially babies. You wouldn't think of taking a child to work at the typical day to day rut job, so don't take them to meetings either!

NEGATIVE SPOUSES

Negative spouses should be left at home. (This includes owner's wives.) A key spouse of one of my upline used some other company's cosmetics and displayed them in her home and in their luxurious hotel suites. I would never put her in front of my group again once I found this out. My oldest stepdaughter once brought home some shampoo and hair conditioner from the beauty shop, products my company made as well, I threw them away with the admonition that in our house we "Played" the game the way we "Said" the game. Chevy dealers should drive Chevys.

CONFLICTING SCHEDULES

When you have conflicting schedules with events, they must be important conflicts such as the wedding of a very close friend or immediate family member, or a unique family event on the same day as a major business event. You don't tell anyone in your downline you can't make it, but explain to your upline the conflict and arrange for them to cover for you.

By telling your downline, you are empowering them to make any excuse in the world not to attend! Encourage everyone to attend every event, no exceptions! Go to great lengths to dramatize your commitment to events. Don't let golf, bowling, fishing, hunting trips, and minor things such as birthdays and anniversaries stand in the way. It isn't popular to take such a stand, but it is vital to make the organization understand how deeply you believe that the event system is an imperative not an option.

BIRTHDAYS, ANNIVERSARIES & HOLIDAYS

Schedule conflicting birthday celebrations before the actual day. Then it really will be a surprise. My children were easy to please and understood the necessity for us to set the pace for the rest of the group to follow. My wife and I celebrated anniversaries and birthdays with vacations to The Islands, Europe and Asia. It certainly was better than a night out at the local version of Denny's.

GUEST SPEAKERS AND TRAINERS

Speakers and trainers have your future in their hands every time they take the stage to speak to your group, or you promote their CDs and DVDs to the group. Treat them like kings and queens. Never take a chance that they might be down.

My upline was a stickler on treating people who came in and spoke to our people well. He insisted they be met at the airport, at the gate, by well-dressed, positive, upbeat leaders in the organization. If their wife was coming the wife of the host was to be with him when they met the speaker.

There was to be flowers and a fruit basket in the room. They were to be pre-checked into the hotel. Special notes and banners proclaiming the expectancy of the group was to be displayed for them. Dexter insisted that treating people first class guaranteed they would want to come back and that they would always say great things about our organization.

Proper protocol means never turning down a work assignment. If you're asked to do something, accept graciously and immediately. Do the job the best you possibly can. I'll never forget my first encounter with the concept of doing "Whatever it takes."

We were at a "Family Reunion" in Hilton Head, South Carolina. I was a young and rising star. I had expected to be given the most cherished job of "hosting the keynote speaker" in one of my upline's events, instead he gave me the job of parking cars. It rained cats and dogs the next day, but I parked six hundred cars and met everyone who came with a smile on my face. I never forgot the standing ovation I received later that weekend when Rick introduced me for an insignificant ten minute speech.

I doubt anyone in my group who saw me that day, wet as a rat, in my best suit; parking cars in the driving rain ever forgot what I did. One thing for sure, no one ever thought any job I asked them to do was beneath them. I've swept floors, taken tickets at the door, picked up speakers, set up sound systems, ran the spot lights, and stood in the flood lights. To me, one was as good as the other because, like the brick layer, I was "Building a cathedral of hope for me and my family."

PLAY AND WORK

I'm a work-a-holic and a play-a-holic. A psychologist friend of mine once said of me "When Bob works he works hard, and when he plays he works harder." I tend to be intense about everything.

The cruel thing about network marketing is that you usually reach "play time" before anyone in the downline does. The tendency is to involve your leaders in your play time. My upline tried to do this to me, I resisted the temptation, opting instead to keep my nose to the grindstone and catch up with them.

Proper protocol says to keep the play time limited to business building events. You can't afford to be a stumbling block to your own group. Unfortunately, I didn't heed this advice and took some of my own downline leaders out of their routines too soon. You will carry a lot of influence, be certain as you get more successful to watch your step.

When you want or need time off, go away with friends or family outside the business. Don't make it too obvious early on in your network marketing career that you are playing at all. Those who are working resent it and may be tempted to play too soon, destroying their chance to have what you have, and putting you back to work rebuilding their group. Work ethics are hard to teach in a nation that is obsessed with leisure and free time.

In smaller events, where someone in your downline is taking the leadership role, it behooves you to get out of the way. It may be advisable for you to leave town for a few days and work with an out of town group. Remember, if you have taught your groups to be at all functions and events, no excuses, and you are in town but don't show up, some will see it as a failing by you. Protocol may say to get out of the way while others get some experience, but it also says don't violate one law while obeying another.

HALLWAY LEADERS

When you are at an event, be there! I've seen too many leaders out in the hallway of a hotel while someone inside is training the group. There are two things wrong with this habit. One is you are not hearing what's being said to your group. Two is you are setting a bad example for those in your downline to follow. Many times leaders use this time as a time to discuss projects with their own leaders. Bad timing! Don't do it! Be visible inside.

Once, while I was training two hundred of his top field leaders, the owner of the company was up in his hotel suite holding court with other leaders. He missed the positive experience being had downstairs by the "many" to listen to the complaints of "a few." Nothing that goes on in the hallways during meetings is worth the negative impact that it leaves.

The following list is but a few of the more important things to consider when addressing the issue of protocols…

1. Always introduce the spouses of speakers and dignitaries.

2. Include the names of key people in the organization when speaking from stage.

3. Provide special name tags for leaders.

4. Give more recognition and stage time to bigger award winners.

5. Lay down rules and don't use anyone in an event that shows up late or is not dressed appropriately for the occasion.

6. Don't ever use people in an event who are involved with the building of another network marketing company.

7. Don't gift wrap gifts to be given from stage. It takes too much time to unwrap and bores the audience.

8. Make everyone feel important.

9. Let people "say" their own name, who their sponsor is and what they did/do for a living... why? Because it edifies those who are building the business and saying one's profession makes people in the audience "identify" people they may know who are in the same profession. It takes away excuses and the fear factor.

Chapter 8

POWERFUL and AFFECTIVE EVENTS

"Let him who wants to move and convince others be first moved and convinced himself."-- Thomas Carlyle

If I've heard it once I've heard it a thousand times, "Why do I have to go to the meetings?" Now mind you it doesn't come from those who have experienced the kind of life changing experience that many of us have had, but rather from those who have sit through a boring dissertation by some statistically overqualified stuffy professorial type or some uninformed fool.

No one likes to sit for hours on end and listen to some pompous, over stuffed person try to dazzle us with numbers, or data which at best is useless and at worst gets in the way of productive behavior. The kind of events that move us to action and provide turning point experiences is the kind of meeting everyone can get excited about.

THE FUNCTION OF FUNCTIONS

Meetings, Events, and Functions. These are the three categories that most companies and industry leaders lump together and call "meetings." There is a very significant difference. The differences are subtle at times.

For example, in all three you would have speakers; you would have an agenda, and an audience. While all "Events" are meetings, all "Meetings" are NOT events.

The similarities end in these generalities. "Meetings" are the basis for new beginnings. Even when you have an "Event or Function" you might have a meeting to discuss the speakers and agenda. Meetings are home trainings, opportunity gatherings, basic training, and planning sessions.

"Events" are bigger. Have a different agenda and a specific purpose. An event is designed to move the group along. It is not designed for those who are not in your business. Some events are designed for those who have accomplished something. For example, those who have sponsored three new frontline this week/month, or those who have attained a certain sales volume over a measured period of time.

"Functions" differ from meetings and events because as the name implies they have a specific function. Usually a function is a weekend or an extended meeting. Functions always include some type of leadership training. Functions are designed to get across advanced ideas in motivation and inspiration. Functions are designed to reveal information not meant for the general distributor population.

Functions may deal with negative in the group, and explore the need to eradicate something that is hurting the organization. Functions must be carefully orchestrated so that they don't backfire. Remember, you are pulling together the power hitters in your group and they could turn on you, so you better have something to give them. I am certain that learning how to do functions effectively may be the hardest thing you'll ever learn.

Meetings, events, and functions all are meant to work in synergy to accomplishing essential things. It is important not to treat them the same. People who don't support meetings and events should not be allowed into your functions. Why… because they are not in sync with the harmony of the entire operation. People who come to functions do so at the invitation of those who are putting the function on. These are not "You all come" meetings. People who come to functions should generally all have a common upline somewhere.

Meetings are open to everyone. The subject matter is kept to uplifting and forward motion information. Lots of recognition! At functions we rarely do formal recognition. Many times there is only one speaker, someone with lots of experience. Sometimes several people share the speaking duties. (A form of recognition) One of the most inspiring and important functions I ever attended was called a "Go-Diamond" function. Four very successful couples shared with the group how they had overcome negatives at home in order to get it "together together" and build a successful downline business.

Everyone who builds a successful business goes through tough times with their spouse or significant other. Knowing how others got through it, or that they actually argued over "investing in the business" (A euphemism for spending the rent money on CDs and DVDs, products, or training). Discussing how to handle financial problems, when to increase life-styles, when to quit your day job, how to counsel others, making it through crisis times of belief. There are so many topics that are covered in functions.

Early in my network marketing career, I attended one of these "Rallies." I must admit to being put-off by some of the "hype" that appeared on the surface. The longer I sat and listened, the more I became convinced that "hype" was sometimes in the eye of the beholder.

We are all guilty at times of bringing our own set of prejudices that can distort our viewpoint. When we look at anything new or strange to our experience, we should keep an open mind and remember that a closed mind cannot learn.

A prejudice is "an unfounded belief." I admit that there are many charlatans in the world who hype their products or declare that their "deal is more rewarding." The bottom line is that when we have something that really is good we should be more excited and cheer more loudly than those whose message is false. The reason the fakers and charlatans get more press is that they do a better job of selling their inferior products and programs.

The lesson to be learned should be to sell louder, longer and more vociferously when you have superior products and programs! Remember, even superior products won't sell themselves. Despite the belief of some, even the good Lord had need of messengers to tell his story.

Events provide this arena. I cannot tell you how excited I was to go to events when I discovered the true reasons for all that went on there.

If you've read my book "Raising a Giant" you know that while I am not particularly a finicky eater, I hate beets. Arnold Swartznegger with an Uzi could not force a beet down my throat! One of the early events held by my upline featured a country and western singer and a dance troop who entertained us with about 10 minutes of clogging. Now, I'm not big into clogging or country music for that matter, but it amused me that at a business meeting we would take up so much time with nothing but pure entertainment. The life insurance companies I had worked for certainly didn't see the need for this nonsense... CLOGGERS?

Some years later while sitting in a leadership event my upline mentor explained that some people come for the music, while others come for the recognition, while some came to learn how to build a successful business. Now everyone got everything. It was his contention that those who came for the music would find the business opportunity and soon become more active in the building of a successful downline. Good thinking! Beets! Something I didn't like or appreciate someone else found exciting and delicious. Every event theme then should be... "Something for Everyone!"

Recognition is one of the biggest elements to building a successful downline organization. Recognition levels are tied to volume, volume is what you get paid on. So recognition is one of the key motivating factors in the size of your income! Without events, how can you make the recognition programs work? Most companies in network marketing are missing this element!

The "System" is built on a strong event system. This means monthly events! Why? You probably get paid for monthly production don't you? Then monthly performance must be measured and rewarded! If you got paid weekly, then weekly events might be in order.

There must be a uniformly recognized level of

progress that moves the mass distributor group to performance! Events are held to inform, motivate, and recognize. Since new people are coming in each month, then formal indoctrination must be held to get them started on the correct pathway to success. The best trainers and motivators from the highest performance group must be available to do this training.

These leaders must have come together to provide a uniform training and business development system. They must have made a long-term commitment to excellence and uniformity.

To be successful, everyone must make the monthly events their highest priority! Events should get bigger and more exciting! To do this requires everyone's attendance!

INVEST IN YOURSELF

Another thing I discovered early in my career in network marketing was that this was a "pay-as-you-go" deal… In other words "no free lunch." This means everyone pays their own way. Since you are in business for yourself, then each one must take their fair share of the expense of putting on exciting and rewarding events!

I've always gladly paid the small amount my upline charged to attend their meetings. Maybe it was because I knew the value from my previous experience in the Life Insurance business, or maybe it was because it was apparent that when someone else pays my way, then I am obligated and no longer free. Explain to your new people what to expect so there isn't any negative reaction when they are confronted at the door with an unexpected expense.

There's absolutely no reason why anyone should have a negative response to paying to get into meetings. What other industry allows you the opportunity to buy successful advice and constructive behavior modification programs on the installment plan? Most industries require massive training fees up-front!

Another way to look at the door charge or training fee issue is what it would cost you to put on meetings and events for your downline should you have to pay for it yourself. It would probably eliminate you from the business altogether.

The "share the cost" as you go plan allows everyone access to the financing required to stage future meetings. This spreads the expenses out so that when it comes your turn to stage events, you can do so without sacrificing your life-style. You can spend more of your bonus checks on life-style instead of spending bonus money to hold meetings.

Get your attitude right toward investing in your business growth, and the attitude of those in your group will improve immensely.

Internet Note:

Thanks to the internet there are massive amounts of information available. Some of this information produces new and better/larger results… some of it is fluff and not worth much. Find a mentor to ferret out as much information as possible and organize it into useful data. Pay for the best and leave the rest… FREE info many times is worth what you pay for it. Don't get sucked in.

EVENTS AND MEETINGS AS PROFIT CENTERS

One of the complaints heard most often in the network marketing world is that of the money made from the sale of books, CDs and DVDs, and tickets to events. What is commonly called "ancillary income." In other words, income that is not directly derived from the sale of the products that your company sells.

"Materials" are things such as audio and video CDs and DVDs, books, and training manuals, or sales aids, and meeting and event fees. Let me make it clear that I believe that business men and women should look for ways to enhance profits when there is a productive and reasonable motive for doing so. I do not believe that unwarranted or unreasonable expenses should be forced on those whose means are limited, and whose naiveté may make them fodder for wolves.

There then are two major considerations here. One is cost and the other is value. I admit that sometimes value is a subjective and hard to determine thing. But common sense tells us that overpaying for information and materials can be a disastrous thing.

Just because we can charge exorbitant fees and get by with it does not justify the practice. However, we should agree that a reasonable profit derived from a beneficial experience is the capitalist way.

Let's face the fact. Some people have a talent for doing something others cannot do. I can't sing, play the piano, or dance worth a darn. (I have references that can vouch for all three.) But I admire those who can, and wouldn't begrudge them the opportunity to make a good living doing what they do for our pleasure and benefit. I am a pretty good speaker and trainer. I have a knack for being able to entertain while getting across dynamic, business related information. Just as the singer and artist should get paid for what they do, I feel I am entitled to make a nice living doing "my thing." (Incidentally, I am available for group events see my blog for more details)

The argument against ancillary income is that the company pays us to recruit, train, and motivate our downlines; therefore anything other than these directly derived commissions is unfair. This is not altogether a weak argument, for certainly part of our compensation is to cover the costs of recruiting and training of our downline.

There is another side however. This side of the equation says that all are not equal in ability or work ethic. I have identified ten distinctly different talents, skills, and attributes necessary to be successful in network marketing. (I cover these in my Leadership I course available online at www.gobobcrisp.com)

It is my firm belief that it is a "combination" of people with compatible talents and objectives that makes for a successful experience in network marketing. If you have four of these skills, and can combine with others to access the other six, then you too can have a successful network marketing experience.

Two of these skills are very rare and hard to access. Who's to say what the missing skills are worth to you or me? The potential income which may accrue to those who possess the skills, or characteristics we lack may well be worth the extra income derived.

The best way to look at this element is to ask the question, how would this be viewed were it in another environment? In other words, if an "outside" speaker/trainer were brought in what would he/she expect in compensation? The same value we place on a Zig Ziglar, Denis Waitley or Tony Robbins then should apply, for the most part, to the value we place on the talents and services of those who have the wisdom and experience to show us the way in network marketing.

Also the issue of sideline or crossline training must be considered. Why should I train someone not in my downline unless I'm getting paid to do so? Charging a reasonable fee for training may be the easiest way to address this issue.

My upline was absolutely clear on the issue of making money on tools and events. He said as long as the opportunity were "available" to everyone, then it was a fair deal… it's hard to argue that point. Certainly those who worked the hardest, and advanced up the ladder more quickly, were more apt to make a significant ancillary income than those who procrastinated, over analyzed and failed to learn the lessons of success.

McDonalds, I am told, charges $40,000 for their franchise training program. Just imagine spending two or more weeks to learn how to manage and maintain a hamburger stand! I've paid thousands for training and have never ever felt that I was robbed or taken advantage of. Sometimes it took years before the training paid off in monetary rewards, sometimes only days, but always the rewards came.

Let's face it making money is an offence to some in and of itself. A college degree can cost over a hundred thousand dollars and have little direct value in the performance of one's chosen occupation. Yet we applaud the attainment of a "Formal" education. Most network marketing educators have something positive to contribute to their student's practical advancement. They have earned the respect of their peers and have the right to expect a monetary reward for their efforts.

Make a commitment now to seek out the best information from the best performers and teachers. Be willing to pay what you can afford even if it hurts a little. Set aside a budget monthly for your personal advanced learning program.

Don't quibble over the price. The price of obtaining knowledge is only exceeded by the cost of not having it!

Learning to feed a giant is about information, powerful information, powerfully presented, dynamically received, and passionately applied!

Tony Robbins asserts that, "It is in our moments of decision that our destiny is shaped!" Decide to grow, expand your knowledge and horizons. Don't be "Penny wise and pound foolish." Don't let anyone steal your dreams, nor for that matter, don't let anyone cheapen them either."

Chapter 9

THE MATURATION PROCESS

"It's a two-way street paved with faith. There's the expectation of top performance in exchange for being provided all the necessary tools."
-- Larry Weisman, USA Today
Concerning the San Francisco 49ers

A prominent industry publication recently ran a story about a "successful" distributor who said that in the six years or so he'd been with his company he had built an organization of "six thousand downline" and that he "could retire right now and never work his business another day." Well he better have a serious day job lined up because with six thousand downline in six years he isn't anywhere near finished!

Why am I surprised at the naiveté of so many in the industry? Has the whole world gone mad or does it just seem that way? Security in network marketing doesn't come with a certain number of downline, (although the number is not six thousand) but with a solidly developed group of successful downline leaders, who are making sufficient income to support their families, and are growing in wisdom and stature. Those who have a long term vision of the growth of their business.

All successful network marketing businesses, and for the moment, let's describe successful as one that provides a full time income for you and your family, come to maturity in stages. These stages are........

1) Immature

2) Maturing

3) Mature.

A network marketing downline needs time to season, to develop staying power, find its place, get comfortable and dig in for the storms that are certain to come.

Immature leaders are usually guilty of thinking that they are further ahead than they really are. It usually comes with a larger than expected bonus check or two. A good thing to remember is that anything that can be built fast can fall fast! The worst mistake to make is to assume the best; the best mistake is to assume the worst. This coincides with my passionate belief that one should "Believe in everyone, and count on no one!"

Stay at it for a few years! My upline taught me the following rule of thumb and I've seen nothing in twenty one years to change my mind about this. He said, you can only "build" three good legs a year. That is, if you are working six days (nights) a week, you can build three good legs a year. (The Internet might change the numbers quite a bit)

If you work three legs, while bringing a few more along in the maturing phase, then the following year you will have three more to work with giving you six good legs. The three from the previous year will need guidance and counseling, taking some of your "building time" the second year, but if you've tied them into "The System," then they will be more "System dependent" than "sponsor dependant." This will leave you free to build three new legs. In time you will have a mature organization!

The graphs illustrate what a new "successful" organization looks like. What it should look like two to three years into the "building process," and then three to five years from that point. Remember, we always draw out our organizations "Left to right," with the strongest leg furthest left, and descending in strength toward the right. Use red and black markers to do this so you can readily identify "new" growth and "rising leaders."

I. Immature Organization Approximately 1 Year Old

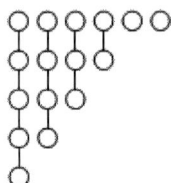

New groups tend to develop very imbalanced toward one strong leg. This is a good thing. "Tap Root" principle at work.

II. Maturing Group Approximately 2-3 Years Old

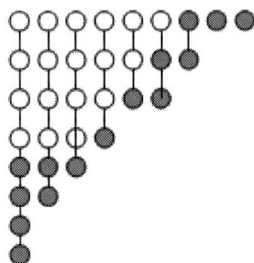

This group is a "healthy" maturing group. Good side to side growth while still developing good depth in legs one through six. This indicates that "new" leaders are emerging.

III. Mature Group Approximately 3+ Years Old

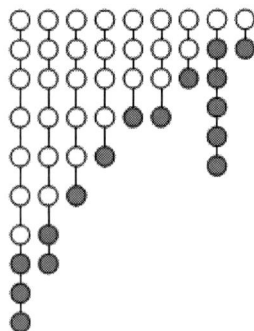

Mature groups usually have someone who comes along later and moves into your "top three". This proves that YOU haven't forgotten how to do it!

Unfortunately no new frontline growth due to new demands on you to manage and lead more.

● New growth on the "Leading Edge"

There has been a popular concept circulating for a few years that "Everyone has a money leg." The indication here is that up to eighty percent of your income will come from one leg. While this may in fact be true of a newly successful achiever, it should not be the case as the group matures. Why? Because people not involved in your "money leg," those you are probably relying on to qualify you for income on your "money leg," are being given second class citizenship in the group... this can create jealousy and involve a great deal of "plate spinning."

No wonder top leaders who promote this concept are always sponsoring new frontline groups, they have to replace the ones they burned out last year trying to keep the income from their so called "money leg" coming in. This may be the most subtly abusive concept to come along in the history of network marketing! I believe it is the result of companies who have designed their bonus plans in the classic old-time "breakaway" style. More recently, it seems companies are going to a combination or "hybrid" style bonus plans which combine the best of a breakaway and "levels based" bonus plans... even new fangled "binary plans" have some interesting twists.

When top level distributors "stretch" too far to reach the maximum bonus pay-out every month, something else has to give. Usually what gives is leadership development and business management. No time is allotted for the ever increasing responsibility of "The System." This requires the best talent to stay in "Phase one" of the business when they should be advancing through phases two through five.

Don't get me wrong, I believe in sponsoring "Width and Depth," but I believe history has proven that those who build for the long haul and work with their downline groups over a period of several years will create more mature, solid, long-lasting businesses!

Rectifying the sins of the past is difficult. Most of these people have gotten used to living on their income from the money leg and therefore cannot afford to go back and build correctly for fear their immediate incomes will suffer. It's a catch twenty-two. If they continue like they are, they will continue to have one strong leg and the rest will be weak. If they give up the immediate income, they may have to cut back their life-style temporarily.

Corporate leadership is constantly pushing the concept of "more width" to their best talent. Not realizing that the people best at sponsoring should be best at teaching others to sponsor also.

Too bad! And very short sighted! The test of leadership and building prowess lies in the number of different legs you can teach, advise, work with, and take to the top level in your company's award system, while creating leaders with full time incomes in the process.

Note: A good solution for some companies might be to declare a "qualification moratorium" in exchange for their top qualifiers concentrating on building their legs two thru six. This would double, triple, and in many cases quadruple volume overnight.

There is a difference between developing talent and discovering talent. No doubt we would all like to think that our best chance for success is to go after existing talent. The truth is that the process of building a successful network marketing group relies on the ability of a company to develop their own talent over time.

When events don't grow in size and volume in legs three and on doesn't increase with time, and then you can bet you're on the treadmill and will likely stay on it.

Maturity takes time, maturing involves a seasoning process… immaturity will destroy everything you've worked and hoped for. Don't be shortsighted! Seek out a mentor who knows how to create a long-term solid business. Don't sell out the future for a comparatively smaller reward today.

GOING FULL-TIME

Going full time too soon can put undue pressure on you and the result can be disastrous. Just as the good farmer knows that some of this year's harvest is for next year's seed, so does the good network marketer know that the first fruit of their labor should be plowed back into the future of their business!

Going full time creates too much pressure on the income side of the business. Most who go full time find their production actually goes down instead of up. (The exception to this may be those who are in business for themselves prior to getting involved)

Financially strained individuals make "money driven" decisions instead of "business driven" ones. The test of whether to go full time or not is simple. Put your paycheck from your job into a savings account for six months. Live entirely on your network marketing bonus check. If your business does not suffer, and your life-style increases without touching your paycheck money, you are probably ready to be full time.

BACKING OUT OF A LEG

The issue of maturity brings with it the issue of when and how to "Back out of a leg." Legs develop around personalities... and blends of styles and temperaments. Each of my legs had a personality. No two of them were the same. You have a certain knack or chemistry with the leaders and general population of distributors in a leg. Care must be taken when changing that mixture.

Unless you relinquish some of the duties to others, you will not be able to build other legs and will be trapped in depth forever. Not a good way to become rich and famous in network marketing. Yet, the timing and the method used to transfer responsibility is just as vital as the fact that you must eventually do it.

There are some constants to consider:

1. Has the volume of new distributors been increasing steadily for six months or longer?

2. Is there someone on your tenth level or deeper, making a full time, solid income from the business?

3. Are there several good leaders who have made an all-out commitment to the business, and have they proven their commitment by their actions over a six to twelve month period?

4. Is there a geographic insulation somewhere in the downline? Have you developed a backup group in another geographic area? (This will protect you from some unseen negative, which could cripple or destroy the leg and put you into the dreaded rebuilding mode.)

Depth, Volume, Income, Geography, and Leadership all contribute to the security of a network marketing leg. If you can answer yes to all of the above, then you probably have a leg that has some reliable staying power. Backing out of a leg then is a matter of quietly scheduling yourself into the leg less and less until you are going into the group only once a month.

Making an announcement that you are decreasing your activity in a leg is a risky and unnecessary act. Most people at higher income levels have lost control of their business. They are jerked around from pillar to post, oiling the squeaking wheel without regard to structure. They've lost control of their calendar and are simply busy being busy.

In spite of all you do, if YOU are the driving force in your business, then you need to realize that your group is counting on you to provide mature guidance and counseling as well as backup support.

Why would someone called to the high calling of leadership ever desire to be free from their life's greatest work? The miracle is you! You are the one who paid the price and now can enjoy the extreme rewards of your work!

In "Raising a Giant," I explained the need to work your depth using the 3-2 concept. Building a mature organization requires concentrated work in depth. Were I working in the popular "Bi-nary" program, I MIGHT work a concentrated "2-2" pattern. Nonetheless I would work depth twice the level of my pay plan!

The reason for working that deep is the "lateral" movement of those in your lower (deeper) tiers. I refer to these people as the "leading edge" of the business. In ALL network marketing companies, fully one-third to one-half of the distributor network is in the process of "evaluation."

They are moving **through** the network not **up** the network. The first order of business is to slow the exodus of new distributors.

Note: If this is not the case with your company or individual downline, then you are simply not putting enough new people into the mill. Retention rates in larger organizations tend to be lower percentage wise. Too high a retention rate usually indicates poor sponsoring habits.

You must always be cognizant of the fact that a very large part of your income relies upon the whim and fancy of a significant number of non-committed members. It can be quite disconcerting to imagine that so much is riding on the decisions of such a transient group. It is imperative to have a solid game plan for getting these undecided votes to go your way.

TOP LEADERSHIP

EMERGING LEADERS

TRANSIENT GROUP
(Less than 90-120 DAYS in the business)

The Leading Edge of your business

PHASE V

PHASE IV

PHASE III

PHASE II

PHASE I

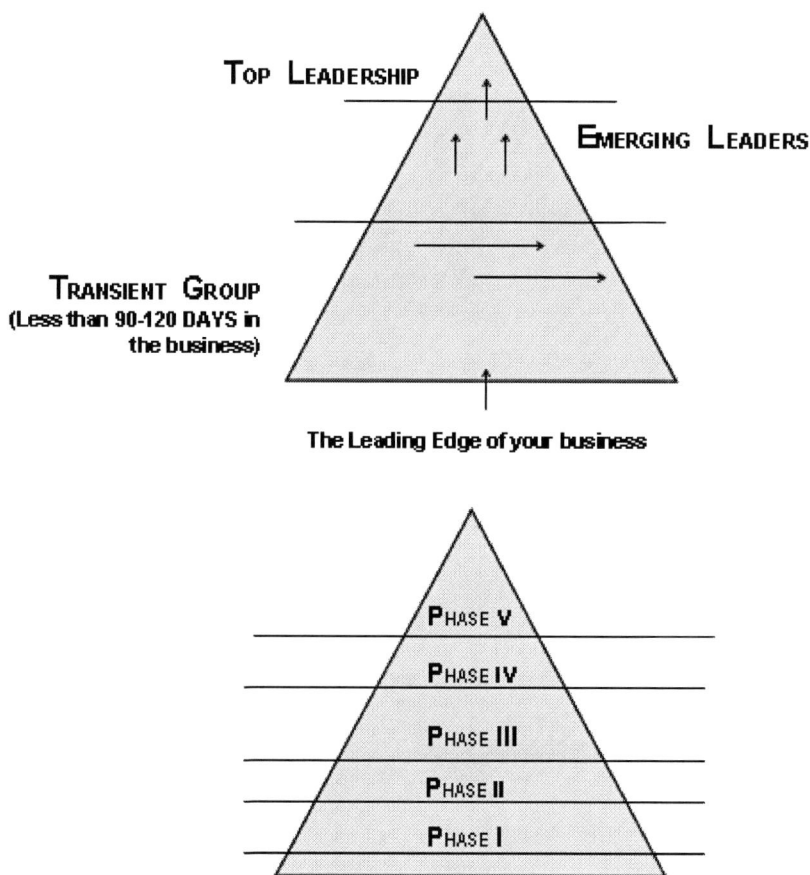

The illustration above will illustrate what I mean by "laterally moving members."

You can best characterize much of this group by simply acknowledging that they are "Coming from Amway, and headed to Herbalife" or whatever, with a brief stopover in your company. You get the picture. Because it takes so little to get started in network marketing, why should new people care much whether it works or not?

What you want is to create programs for sifting through this river of humanity to find those who have a genuine interest in your opportunity and eliminating those who are insincere and are wasting your time.

The System will help you identify the ones you want... these are the ones who will develop and thrive in your program. These people are sometimes hard to identify and will take a really comprehensive program to attract them.

We live in dynamic and changing times. Once Amway and Shaklee dominated the network marketing landscape. They could take years to identify and develop their talent. Today we are given a few months, at best, to get someone focused and on track. The baby-boomers are aging and are impatient. They want results quickly, want to be educated and motivated by someone who knows what they're doing, not someone who has had six months experience and is still trying to figure it out themselves.

PERPETUAL IGNORANCE

Traditionally, those who came into your company from someone's warm market were content with allowing their friend to dictate the learning curve and drive the success pace. Today the new warm market member is more likely to look to someone more successful and who has more experience. This means getting new people "plugged in" to the upline. This, hopefully, avoids the pitfall of "perpetual ignorance."

Consider this. Six to eight friends get into your business in a continuous chain straight down. They all have been in for less than five to six weeks. Who's the leader?

Answer? No one! They're all babes. How can you turn their success over to them? No industry in the world asks their participants to succeed without proper preparation. The only way to slow down the exodus, find the winners, and those serious about your business, is to teach your members the importance of "The System." This means EVENTS, RECOGNITION, AND TRAINING/TOOLS. This is where you find the future leaders!

Avoid complacence. No one is good enough to ignore the need for a new supply of faces to populate the ever increasing leadership void. Polish up your style. Put your best foot forward. Creating new habits will create new excitement. Doing away with self-defeating practices and putting the emphasis on excellence, will create a new culture that will last. Good wine needs time to ferment, to mature, to grow in boldness and taste. Good organizations need the same.

When you asked your downline for loyalty, you must expect that they will require the same from you. I once had a prospective buyer of a network marketing company that I represented, asked me if he could "count on me being in the deal regardless the extent of my personal loss," my reply to him was to ask him if he were willing to commit the entire fortune that he possessed to the extent that he was homeless to the deal. He laughed and told me he would not. I told him I could not commit to him what he was not willing to commit to himself. He obviously was not a very good leader of men. Foxhole generals turn my stomach, how about you!

SUMMARY

I.   The worst mistake to make is to assume the best; the best mistake is to assume the worst.

II. There is a difference between developing talent and discovering talent.

III. The baby-boomers are aging and are impatient. They   want results quickly, but want to be educated and motivated by someone who knows what they're doing, not someone who has had six months experience and is still trying to figure it out themselves.

Chapter 10

LIVE THE DREAM

"A man's gotta have a dream. If we can dream it we can do it." -- Jim Valvano (deceased) North Carolina State Basketball Coach - Winner

This chapter focuses primarily on the material dreams that each of us have. Even Mother Theresa had to raise money to feed the poor. I have fought since childhood to understand the controversy over material riches, and still do not know why good people work all their life for so little.

The late Dr. Norman Vincent Peale used to say that "The world will give you, for the most part, what you asked for." Why ask for so little? I've usually found that those who have little are the fondest of what they have. Proud to be humble and broke I guess.

Here we'll take an honest look at dreams and expectations. I trust the reader will understand that I make no apologies for success. Mine or others… I also trust that the reader will grant that giving is a private affair and therefore not discussed in these pages. People who make a big deal out of what they give to charity or church are hypocrites, and as the Good Book says, "Have their reward." That's enough.... Now let's dream!

Why is it that people have the innate power to find the

wrong? Something which draws them toward destructive behavior? Why can't we focus on the positive instead of the negative? Teaching others to let go and dream again is the hardest challenge we may confront. To inspire positive reaction in the mass of our downline, we must learn to live the dream.

Too many so called successful distributors in network marketing companies are trying to convince us they are successful while driving an old car, wearing out of date clothes, and a ten dollar watch, that indicates otherwise. They don't dress the part, act the part, or live the part. Ask any woman and she'll tell you that nothing lifts your spirits like a new outfit.

The average person sees a new Ferrari go down the road and they stare until it is out of sight. They don't stare at a two year old Chevy Suburban or a brand new Toyota truck, but they stop dead in their tracks when an exotic sports car or new Mercedes Benz goes by. Most wouldn't dare dream of owning a Rolls Royce (or Roller as they're called in London) or a Bentley Azure, but would point and stare at each that passes.

What is it with the idea that we are no longer impressed with wealth? Not so! When network marketing leaders demonstrate their success, the man on the street sits up and takes notice. I'm not talking about outrageous consumption, or contending that you should ignore common sense and tasteful behavior. I'm talking about showing the world how they can live if they pay the price to have it. What's more impressive, someone showing a big check or driving up in a new Benz?

To me the person showing the check may or may not

have class, but the person in the new Mercedes is showing me he/she has taste and substance! A cheap pair of shoes, inexpensive suit and tie, or tacky dress, only says that you don't have the success or good taste to afford better.

Dream vacations can be a big turn on to your downline. Most people dream of going to exotic places. When you can afford it, you should schedule a dream vacation. Carry a digital camera and take pictures of everything. Put your story on your computer and the internet and show them to your downline. Demonstrate what being successful means. It will inspire others to achieve what you have achieved!

Note: Carry a cell phone with a camera and use it to take photos of people at a meeting or event … make one with your upline and send it to them right on the spot.

It's true that some people are not into "things," but most of us want to drive a nice new car, wear designer clothes, and have a beautiful home. People who run around flaunting checks are bores who usually have no class and aren't relatable to most of us.

The real lesson here is to go with the main stream flow on issues that relate to symbols of success. You may indeed like a Ford truck better than a 500 SL, but they sell many more pickups than 500SLs wonder why? Chose not to be ordinary!

We're all impressed by money, but it's the things that money will do that means the most to us. Money in the bank is nice, but it can't be seen and verified. Even money that is given away has a large impact.

So called "little dreams" such as having enough money to have your nails done every week, or to afford a maid to come in once a week to clean your house thoroughly may be the most important in the beginning. Hiring someone to mow the lawn, buying a new swimming pool for the kids, or taking the whole family to Disney World or Hawaii may be the thing that moves your group to the next level.

Teach people to teach others about dream building. Imagine having your whole leadership group taking people out on weekends to look at new homes, luxury cars, or nicer furniture. Stop by a travel agency and pick up some travel brochures to share at the weekly training meeting.

Note: Send links to websites or web pages that depict the dream vacation of the week… use technology to convey the possibilities that exist.

Schedule someone to speak on exotic travel destinations, or borrow or rent a film on some popular destination! If your company or upline is sponsoring a trip somewhere, get plenty of pictures and promote it to everyone!

Timing is everything. No other industry puts the emphasis on life-style changes as much as network marketing. Always remember who is watching you.

Plan life-style changes to coincide with attained goals. Demonstrate that even the smallest goals are important. Have people share with the group at each meeting the things that are happening in their lives as a result of building a successful business.

While life-style changes usually have a positive effect, they can also have a negative effect at times. Under "normal" business growth situations, most people would celebrate your new found success. At other times, under abnormal conditions, they might actually be turned off.

I bought a two million dollar jet just before the downturn of my business. I thought I was setting a good example for everyone by expanding my life-style to even greater heights. (I already owned several exotic cars, a multimillion dollar home and had a closet full of expensive clothes) The jet seemed to be a good challenge to the group.

It backfired, because the leaders in my group were being confronted with cutting back their life-styles due to a downturn in our business growth (A phenomenon that happens to most everyone eventually) as their incomes declined, they resented the fact that my income had not changed. (It took me seven years to find out why my upline had suggested upline counseling before major purchases)

Had I been more aware and taken a more restrained approach, I might have foreseen the need to cut back a little and put myself in a better position to help them out.

Having said that, I firmly believe that prudent and wise investment in life-style is for the benefit of the entire business. On weekends, people in my downline would drive by my house and bring prospects and new distributors to prove the point that someone had in fact "Made it."

I held regular open house events for everyone in the group. The group will take pride in your success; you owe it to them to demonstrate the positive life-style changes that success can provide. It also helps to share in the success, so that each takes personal pride in the accomplishment. I always let top leaders drive my cars, try on the clothes, take pictures with all "The Toys."

My upline advised that a car was the first and most important business building life-style change that we could make. His logic was simple; more people see your car than see your house or bank account. It's something you use every day and it will impact you and your group most. Jewelry and clothes were next on the list for the same reason, then house and vacations followed.

Always this advice was tempered with two admonitions. One, don't go in debt over your head just to impress someone, and two, don't sacrifice your ability to afford to go to events and supply your group with business building materials.

This is a good time to revisit one other very important element in the life-style changes department... retirement from your rut job. The high pressure environment that we live in today often presents a rush to "go full time." The problem with going full time too soon is that most people have never been in business for themselves, and they lack the discipline to handle the lack of a boss to tell them what to do daily. We usually see their network marketing businesses go backwards after retirement.

Also, the money coming in from your network marketing business is "Plus money," this means life-style money. Money to go on trips with the family, build a room on to the house, buy new furniture, hire a maid or gardener or both. This extra money becomes bill paying money when you quit your job. It no longer "takes the pressure off," but instead now that you've retired you have the added pressure of "having" to sponsor and sell. You'll make pressurized decisions that may not be wise. Think twice before advising someone to go full time.

A good rule of thumb for making the commitment to be full time is to take your income from your job, put it in a savings account for six months, and live on your network marketing income only during this time. If you can afford your normal payments, finance the growth of your business without borrowing, and have a visible increase in your standard of living, then you're ready. If not keep the day job!

Chapter 11

THE GREAT DEPTH DEBATE

"Negative feedback is meant to correct forward motion, not stop it." -- Anthony Robbins

Most full-time network marketers are successful simply because they persist. It isn't so much that they work smart, but they simply do more than others who do not succeed. Certainly, much of my success was attributable to shear effort. I don't believe anyone can truly succeed in life without a determined effort. However, having said that, I am also very certain that were I given some more direct guidance in the early stages of my career, I could have saved a lot of heartache and miles on my body.

There is no more misunderstood concept in network marketing than the concept of "working depth." As I have related earlier, the concept of "Structure" is foreign to many, but "structure" determines the ultimate growth rate of an organization.

Explosive growth occurs when certain circumstances, some of which we can control, exists. One of the things we can control is the structure of our depth. First, let's discuss what we mean when we say "working depth."

Depth is the word used to describe what we do when we work downline under those on our first level or frontline.

110

There are two schools of thought in network marketing… they are "The Domino Theory" and "The Depth Theory."

The Domino Theory states simply that you "find" leaders you don't "build" leaders. The Domino Theorists point out that it is easier to find a leader than it is to try to build one. Their philosophy is headlined by the motto "throw enough on the wall and some of it will stick." It works I admit it. Anyone who will see several hundred people a month, and share the business opportunity in a proper manner can make this theory work for a while.

The Domino proponents de-emphasize meetings, events, and tools. They have no system to follow. They exhort everyone to stay in the process of sponsoring frontline all the time. They develop anemic groups of individualists. Their loyalty is to their check. If their check goes down they find a new company or new downline. No company is safe for the long haul when their top field leaders teach this philosophy.

The main problem is that you're going against typical numerical expansion or exponential growth patterns. Very simply, the base (depth) of the pyramid is larger than the top!

The "Domino Theory" is an "effect," not a "method" for building a solid business. It is true that the odds are with you the more you sponsor self-starters and people with self-discipline, great self images, and extraordinary skills with people. However, these are people that you will "find" in depth as a result of working the tap root of any leg. Once you find the leader, the "domino effect" begins to work. The difference? Now you have a supporting cast to work with and to build volume, bonus checks, and future leaders.

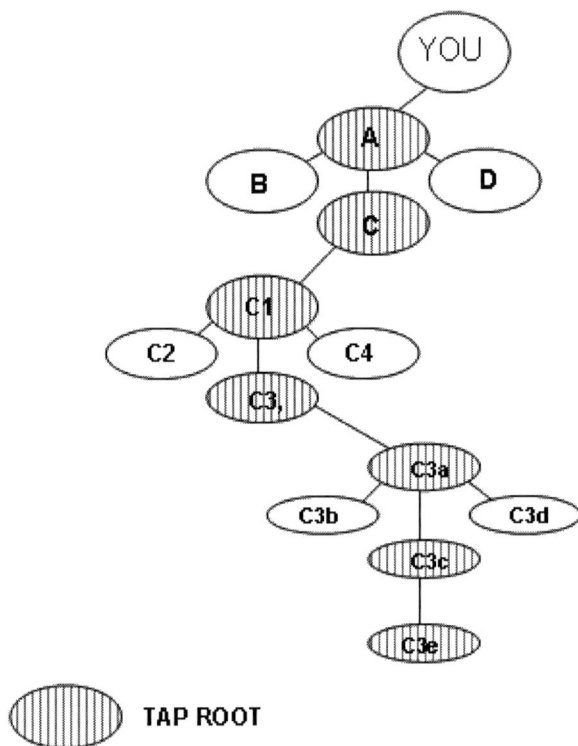

TAP ROOT

The effectiveness of the depth theory lies in the availability of a well-balanced and complete "system" to support those who don't enter into the business with well-honed skills, good self-esteem, and confidence. Most do not possess good work habits, self discipline, or the ability to commit time and energy immediately.

Working depth requires some understanding of the process. If you haven't read my book "Raising A Giant," this would be a good time to get it and reread the chapter called "The Upline Powerline." This will give you a basis for understanding "Who's who in the zoo." Knowing who to look to and expect help from is vital. It will tell you who's looking to you and what is being expected of you.

Working depth properly requires some coordination and cooperation with your own upline.

The theory of working depth is simply that by driving down deep, you are cementing those you are working with or under into the business. Long before any commitment is felt or made, these people have a downline on which they may find an income developing. Some people have tried to shortcut this concept by "stacking" their own prospects under people downline. The only time I think this is advisable is when you are working cold market leads and the person(s) you are stacking under are participating in the cost of generating these leads.

The idea of working depth is not to take your own prospect list and work downline, but to take the prospect list of those new members in depth, and assist them in sponsoring their friends and family. This is known as the "Endless chain" of prospects. Everyone knows someone who needs more money, better health, or is looking to transition to another career.

Working depth also makes it possible to earn while you learn. My sponsor did all of my initial meetings. As a matter of fact, I made him guarantee me that I would never have to do meetings myself. His response was to tell me that he would never ask me to do a meeting I didn't "want" to do. It was obviously a ploy to get me involved and to get to my warm market list. It worked!

Working depth means you get to learn how to do meetings and sharpen your skills on someone else's prospects. (That may mean someone upline is sharpening their skills on your prospect list.) In "Raising a Giant" I cover the role of the "A," "B," and "C" players.

The "A" player takes the lead in depth. He/She directs traffic so to speak in the tap root. A good "A" player will take the tap root down at least one level every week or four to six levels a month. Initially, it is not as important how many people are getting in, as it is how many new generations / levels are added.

By personally working depth the "A" player is guaranteeing themselves a stable and long-term income. Later I will discuss the "Stratification of Influence."

Working depth requires one thing ... focus. Don't become distracted. It's easy to get batted around like a ping pong ball. Everyone wants you to do everything. Impossible! This means plugging the sideline legs (Those not directly in the tap root) into a "system" of events, and using "feeder" meetings for sideline growth. With these meetings and events, and with good training manuals, and tape recorded training and motivational sessions, everyone can be successful!

THE 3-2 CONCEPT

Previously, I covered my depth strategy for binary or matrix type programs. Here we will examine a more traditional strategy for working with mainstream breakaway and uni-level type programs.

The strategy is simple. Build a continuous line downward until you have backed a leader up with a leader. When working downline, your objective in getting someone started is to get them three wide and at least two deep in one of the three legs. This "two deep" leg then is the "leading edge" of the tap root. (See Diagram)

Sometimes you will reach an impasse. The person in depth you are working with has a weak list, no list, or is such a flake their friends and family won't speak to them. Your options are to:

1. To work in the cold market to get going again (Running ads, mailers, flyers, and especially emarketing)

2. To "reverse back up" the line of sponsorship to select a better pathway to depth (The reason we attempt to get three wide),

3. To stack or place one of your own leads under them,

4. Cry in your milk, suck your thumb, pout, get negative and quit.

I always kept in touch with the people between me and the "leading edge," (where my focus was), because I knew the possibility was great that I would need to "backup" the line-of-sponsorship some, to find another avenue to build deeper. Also, once the tap root takes root, you need the people upline for volume and explosive growth. This is why a systematic recognition program is essential and without events you cannot dramatize growth, nor excite the mass to move.

When you work the tap root it is easier to get those upline to go to functions, buy CDs and DVDs, and use the products. Why? Because if they don't, someone in their downline will pass them up, get more recognition, have a bigger check or get advanced training they may not yet be qualified for. Most of us have a built in, keen sense of competition. This competitive spirit makes for a dynamic and explosive situation.

To take advantage of this, you must build personal relationships with those deepest from you. My (sixth person) upline invited me to his house, called me every week to see how things were going, and made me feel special even when it seemed to me that I didn't deserve all the attention. There is a good lesson to be learned here don't miss it. Pay attention to those deepest from you. They are the ones to whom you look for security.

I was taught, and fully believe, that the way to a solid business is to work a proper mixture of width and depth. When the "domino effect" kicks in, you will find it more explosive if you have been working and teaching depth properly. Network marketing groups explode from the bottom up, not the top down.

WIDTH IN DEPTH

You may, by now, be asking yourself, what happens to the entire sideline (Width in depth) that you are passing up to work depth? The answer is simple "The System." Here's where most companies and field leaders miss out. Realizing that it is impossible to work directly with everyone, their answer is essentially to work with no one (The Domino Theory). If you don't create expectancy for good training and systematic development of leaders, then there can be no disappointment when none is forthcoming.

The challenge is that most of these people create an expectation of help while delivering little, if any help at all. The animosity that this created carries over into every aspect of the business.

What do you do if you are caught in one of the sideline legs, one of the legs where the upline "A" player is not working directly? First let me say that this is not where you want to be period. Having said that... let me remind you that I found myself in this exact position. The leg I found myself in was already secured before I arrived on the scene. This meant I had to initially settle for the attention of my sponsor and another upline high level "B" player.

This didn't create a problem in the beginning since most of the basics I initially needed were easily taught by someone who had a good knowledge of the product line, administrative procedures (How to do paperwork and order products), and knew how to explain the bonus plan. Even though their skills with people were lacking, as far as advanced leadership techniques were concerned, they were competent teachers in the lower level trainings.

It didn't take long though for me to outgrow their ability to teach and train me. I found that I had to build on my strengths, create some excitement around me, so that I could get the attention of someone who could help me advance at the pace I wanted to go.

This meant going to meetings once a month that were

held seventeen hundred miles from me. By showing my commitment to "come get the information," I was able to convince a bonafide "A" player to come to Tulsa and teach and motivate my group. Leaders don't wait; they launch out and make something happen.

I also relished the idea of having the area to myself to build a "System" sponsored event. This meant that the rest of the successful people around the company would have to acknowledge my role in the building of an "undeveloped area."

It was probably more of an ego thing than an actual business building requirement. It is better to have no training than the wrong training. I found that at least I could control my own destiny and could see that the growth patterns created by my upline "A" player were preferable to those provided by my immediate upline who lived in my area.

You must "insulate" your group from weak and uncertain trainers / leaders. This does not mean that you "isolate" yourself and the group, because to isolate means to cut yourself off from vitally needed information and participation by someone other than yourself who is dedicated and committed to the success of the business.

TRIGGERING THE EXPLOSION

Once you have driven the depth of a leg down through the tenth generation, and moved the passing parade of transients out of your payline, you are ready to push the volume and sponsoring to a new and explosive level.

What most companies call "momentum" is nothing more than the automation of the domino effect. It usually takes place as a result of finding someone in depth that wants the business passionately and is ready to go now! This person(s) takes charge, learns quickly, takes action immediately and does everything they're asked to do with enthusiasm and passion.

The result is an immediate shock wave that roars through the upline (Those between you and the lion) and creates a rush to "do something quick lest we be left behind!" Remember people do things for only two reasons 1) Opportunity for gain and 2) Fear of loss. This has both those elements in it! Wow! It doesn't get better than this! Remember, HEAT RISES!!!!

The key is knowing how to create the maximum hope for gain, and at the same time inundate them with the fear of loss. Unfortunately, most people are more motivated by fear of loss than they are the opportunity for gain.

Your company's awards programs, pin system, printed recognition, and events will feed this frenzied activity. If your company or upline doesn't have "THE SYSTEM," then you will need to access it yourself!

Proper recognition builds volume! Volume builds checks! Checks create life-style changes! Life-style changes reinforce belief systems! Reinforcing belief systems creates more activity and so the cycle repeats.

Goal setting with dynamic and immediate deadlines is the key. People must have a sense of urgency about their performance level. No urgency creates a "manana" attitude. This means no explosive growth. W. Clement Stone used to have a sales meeting every morning at 7 AM with his agents. He would reward those who did a good job the day before with cash bonuses, trips, plaques, and applause. He would then have them stand and sing rousing sales songs. Then he would tell them what the objectives and rewards were going to be today. By doing this every day he created an immediate and continuous atmosphere of accomplishment!

Great events create urgency. Most of you get paid monthly, this means monthly events filled with recognition. It probably wouldn't be a good idea to ask everyone to get up and show their bonus checks from the previous month. (The legal community frowns on that)

Herbalife was successful at asking those who made over a certain amount to stand up, then asked them to be seated as gradually they moved the amount up. They did this on national television along with their weight reduction recognition. It was potent and effective!

The past has proven it is better to use award levels than to use income numbers. For one thing, the legal community doesn't like us telling our incomes and when we do so today we must, by law, use all kind of disclaimers. So stick with pin recognition. Like Art Williams (Billionaire founder of A.L. Williams Insurance) says "We give away Plaques the size of doors, and trophies the size of men."

Explosive growth just doesn't "happen" there are conditions which have been created that make explosive growth a possibility.

Growth that can be orchestrated can be replicated!

This is good news and should encourage you to work

hard at building the proper "structure" into your business as well as make you an ardent and vocal supporter of "The System " These elements are intertwined and cannot be separated without giving up security and long-term sustained growth for an unreliable means of counting on good luck to create your future.

MEASURING GROWTH

Most people measure growth by the size of their sales volume and the size of their bonus checks. While these are certainly important measuring sticks, they are not however, the ones that will create greater sales volume and larger bonuses. By the time you see your volume and bonus check the time has passed for measuring the health and prospects of growth for your business.

Sales volume and bonuses are the "results" of something else. Think for a moment on what sales growth is a result of? Is it not the result of many things? A good attitude, good training, and proper planning? Strong work ethic (Or weak one?) Isn't your bonus check really a reflection of what has gone on in the months and weeks before? If you agree that this is true, then your measuring stick should be something other than sales volume or bonuses shouldn't it?

How about attendance at meetings and events? Is your weekly meeting stagnant? Boring? Ineffective? Flat line meetings and event are a result of three things.

1) Lack of activity between weekly meetings.

2) No new information or excitement to inspire

continued attendance.

3) Lack of visionary leadership to challenge growth

4) Meeting agendas have become irrelevant … get in touch with the social media… facebook, youtube, myspace, twitter… and use modern technology!

How about movement of books, CDs and DVDs and materials? These ALWAYS precede growth! How about beginning a database (start collecting email addresses) then you can compare attendance, number of guests, who brought guests, and send a nice video email thanking them for their attendance and inviting them back… how neat we can use the internet to create some much needed "High Touch" don't you think?

To get bigger you've got to get better! When meetings and events stop growing the leaders stopped growing long before.

Chapter 12

HAWKS, CHICKENS, DOVES, AND EAGLES

"A society of sheep, must in time, begat a government of wolves." -- Bertrand de Jouvenal

A very successful distributor for one of the industry's largest companies has a leadership training program that he calls, "Dip, Suck, and Pop." Now, the theory here is that the network marketing industry is basically a rip-off deal anyway so ethics and rules are for someone other than him.

Dip, Suck and Pop as it's been explained to me means. "Dip down deep, beyond your payline, Suck someone in depth up to your frontline by using a new ID number, and Pop them out as your own." In other words, rob from your own downline to create new width and income for yourself.

This "strong gets stronger by preying on the weak" practice is a dangerous and destructive concept. It should result in the banning of its practitioners from participating in any way in the industry! There are few practices that I believe deserve the "death penalty" (No longer allowed to participate) more.

When I entered the life insurance industry in 1969, I

was told that there was a code of ethics that we were expected to maintain, and that violating this code could cause me to lose my license. In the network marketing industry, and certainly within the context of any company, there should be a code of conduct as well. In simple terms it is "do unto others." But further and more complex than this is the obligation that each participant has to assure the on-going health of the industry itself.

Every "strong organization" is made up of several smaller weak ones. The business can be very fragile and relies totally on the recruitment of new talent. One of the largest companies in our industry published figures which revealed that their turnover rate exceeded one hundred and twenty percent annually!

The recruitment of new distributors then is the most circumspect of all activities. Remember first that the main customer of every network marketer is the people in your downline. We should do everything possible to protect and preserve the relationship with that person and their upline. This means protecting the line-of-sponsorship.

Healthy competition within the industry and within your own company can be good. It can even be beneficial when implemented properly in expanding business within your own downline. It becomes destructive when upline leaders take advantage of unsuspecting members. The chickens should beware of the hawks! The hawks feed themselves first every time. Eagles feed their offspring first, then eat what is left.

One of my early mentors had a policy that I thought was a good one. He told us if it ever came to a dispute, whether a dime for him or a dollar, he would give us the dollar and take the dime. Why? Because he understood that being "Penny wise and pound foolish" was not in anyone's best interest. You don't "win" arguments and disagreements with your own downline. It comes back to the question, "Would you rather be right or effective?"

At whose expense did you prove your point or feather your own nest? While your success relies at first on YOUR ability to perform, it relies long-term on your downline's ability and willingness to perform. This means that you must maintain a strong sense of ethical behavior in order to secure your future.

Sometimes the rules in your company may allow you to do something that common sense and good ethics may tell you is wrong. For example, when I did larger opportunity meetings it was not unusual for someone to come up to me afterwards and ask me to be their sponsor. The conversation would go something like this:

Prospect: "That was a great presentation tonight, I'm new here and haven't signed up yet, the person that invited me met me in a mall and I barely know him. I frankly don't think he is the right sponsor for me. Would you be my sponsor?"

Now, in most companies I could sponsor him and be well within the "rules." (If this were you would you sponsor him?)

Answer: My answer to someone who confronted me with this dilemma was always: "I'm very flattered that you asked, however, before I answer, let me ask you what you would want me to say when, if I agree to become your sponsor, and do meetings for you, someone like you, asks me to sponsor them, instead of being sponsored by you?" I have yet to have someone who didn't know the correct answer to this question.

FARMING

"Farming" one company to expand your business in another has become a common practice in our industry. These "Chicken Hawks" are a blight and cancer on our industry. This practice violates every ethical and morally sound precept known to man!

The practice of "farming" occurs when someone comes to your meetings, may actually join your business, with the primary intent of meeting people to recruit into another network marketing company.

This is a dishonest and screw worm practice, and should be stopped. If someone approaches you or anyone in your meetings with another opportunity, they should be immediately asked to leave, and if they don't then you should call security and have them ejected.

The Marine Corps has as a motto "Always vigilant." This is a good motto for all of us who value our freedom to practice our businesses without unethical interference.

INVENTORY LOADING

Another practice that needs to stop is the unbridled loading of product (inventory loading) on unsuspecting new members. Now I'm not against having products to "use, show, and sell," but I am against loading someone who cannot afford it, with products they can't use, or sell within a reasonable period of time, and with minimal help from their upline.

While inventory loading is unlawful in most states, the practice continues. Buying product to reach the next discount or recognition level needs to meet the same criteria. Can you reasonably expect to use or sell the products in time to pay the bill created to buy them? (Assuming you used a credit card to buy them.)

My upline use to say… "you can't load a wagon from an empty cart" and I agree. Watch what you do to your downline they will do the same as you when given the opportunity. I always felt the advice I would give my mother is the advice I should be willing to give to anyone.

Someone once bragged, in an Executive Diamond Counsel meeting I was attending in Switzerland, that the leader in one of their key legs pawned silver that had been in the family for decades just so they could qualify for a pin level. This would in turn qualify this couple for the Executive Diamond Counsel. This is unconscionable and should not be tolerated!

Abuse in any form is still abuse! There is a fine line at times between "stretching" and "breaking." All of us need to reach a bit beyond ourselves to grow. Use great wisdom when advising others. Practice the real Golden Rule and you too will have the gold!

SUMMARY

Practice ethical behavior, be vigilant in the defense of others' rights. Beware of these abuses.

1. Stealing prospects and sales from downline or crossline.

2. Farming, neither do it nor condone it… this means "NO passing out business cards at meetings… PERIOD!

3. Inventory loading. Use wisdom and caution when selling products in large quantities to anyone.

4. Never allow someone to do something that would violate good ethical practices just to help someone else attain a goal.

ATTENTION LEADERS

I have an annual Leadership Conference. It's FREE to attend… you will be able to stay current on Technology… what's happening and "Who's Who" check my website for details. www.gobobcrisp.com.

Chapter 13

THE STRATIFICATION OF INFLUENCE

"You reach outward destinations through an inward journey." -- Deepak Chopra

Not only is building a business important, but building one that has built in "fail-safes" is also important. I have always looked at ways to insulate myself and my leaders from unseen negatives and things which could wipe out several years of hard work. My mentor's advice was to "build it once." I have done my best to teach my downline organization to do likewise.

Many times the thing that determines the staying power of a group relies upon their inability to take their groups to another deal. This may mean dividing the loyalty and building the business back to you and your reliable and committed upline.

People rely upon the influence of their immediate upline to determine their continued performance in your business. If you are my best friend and I sponsor you into my downline, the chances are you are going to do what I do. If I get excited and stay excited, then you are likely to do the same. However, if I get negative and quit, you are likely to follow me and quit as well.

My friend's friend, your third level is likely to follow me as well; however, by the time you reach the fourth level of your business, you are now moving out of my "superior center of influence" through to another "level or strata of influence."

These "stratas" are important in that they provide back up positions for each person in the upline. Negative attitudes destroy fragile organizations. When you are working through several stratas of influence, you are "insulating" or protecting yourself and your business by building depth properly.

Now contrast the use of the "Stratification of Influence" with someone who practices the" Domino Theory" of building. They must rely upon the continued good will and whim of those that are "dominoed in" their downline. A dangerous and reckless decision. If the first strata collapses, the second will follow and so on. In other words the dominoes begin to fall backwards instead of forward as intended or desired.

When you work depth properly, you will move through the first, second, and third stratas into the fourth strata where you can be confident you are protecting yourself as well as possible from outside negative influence as well as inside apathy.

Moving from a lethargic strata of influence, to one more convicted and dynamic is every builders goal. Paying attention to who has the most influence in each stratum will be very important to your ability to create long term loyalty and stability.

I know this may sound like a clandestine way to build your business but reality is reality. We are in an industry that attracts those who have very little invested. When your future is at stake it is unwise to trust the newest member's commitment level to secure it.

Look at it this way; you spend hundreds of hours working with a group, only to have someone's brother-in-law suggest that some other network marketing opportunity might be a better deal. The person you sponsor leaves and takes his/her entire downline with them. How do you feel? Sick right? Betrayed right? How about naive or stupid? Shame on you, you relied on your gut instead of human nature.

This won't happen to you more than once before you heed my advice and work down to your fourth strata of influence and then build strong friendships and make your influence felt.

Chapter 14

TEACHERS TEACHING TEACHERS TO TEACH TEACHERS TO TEACH

"Focus on time telling, not clock building."

-- James Collins

"Some people study the roots... others pick the fruit."

■ Jim Rohn

The backbone of the network marketing industry lies in the ability to transfer ideas and concepts to a large number of downline members. This transference begins somewhere in your upline and has no ending. Each person in the teaching / learning chain is both a student and a teacher. This puts a lot of pressure on each link in the chain.

Just as a chain is only as strong as its weakest link, so it is in network marketing. Concepts and ideas get distorted, altered slightly with each transfer, until what's being taught is nothing like the original message.

A continuous, uniform message must be given at all times. Dr. Robert Schuller, the pastor of the Crystal Cathedral, says, "A commitment to continuity produces emotional stability." Since we all desire an emotionally stable and growing business, we must do everything we can to produce an easily replaceable message.

A major reason for a "system driven" tape program is that the tape says the same thing every time. It tells the same message to the person on your frontline that it tells to the one on the tenth level. No deviation. No human error.

Programs which draw the net of information tighter and check our "tone" are vital. We've all known someone who had "perfect pitch" (musically). The truth is that most who claim to have perfect pitch actually have "relative pitch." That is, if you give them middle C on the piano or with a pitch pipe, they can give you a b flat or a sharp or some other desired note. Barber Shop quartets use a pitch pipe to tune them up before a song.

In network marketing, we are always challenged with the problem of "tuning or retuning" the message so that it remains constant and uniform.

Just as the previous chapter dealt with the "Stratification of Influence," an encouragement to work through four stratas of depth, so we are going to address the teaching/duplication process through four generations or levels of depth.

It is vital to understand that "Leadership" chains, and "Sponsorship" chains can be quite different. You may have someone on your first level who takes up the leadership and teaching responsibilities, but it may be another four, five, or six levels further, before you reach the next person who constitutes the "second" leadership level in that leg.

I clipped the following out of a magazine many years

ago and have found it very useful in helping others to learn how to teach what is being taught and not some altered version of the original.

MISCOMMUNICATION

"Don't garble the message!" If I heard that once during Marine boot camp, I must have heard it four dozen times. Again and again, our outfit was warned against hearing one thing, then passing on a slightly different version. You know, changing the message by altering the meaning a tad. It's so easy to do, isn't it? Especially when it's filtered through several minds, then pushed through each mouth. It is amazing how the original story, report, or command appears after it has gone through its verbal metamorphosis.

Consider the following:

A colonel issued this directive to his executive officer:

Tomorrow evening at approximately 2000 hours, Halley's Comet will be visible in this area, an event which occurs only once every seventy-five years. Have the men fall out in the battalion area in fatigues, and I will explain this rare phenomenon to them. In case of rain, we will not be able to see anything, so assemble the men in the theatre and I will show them films of it.

Executive officer to company commander:

By order of the colonel, tomorrow at 2000 hours, Halley's Comet will appear above the battalion area. If it rains, fall the men out in fatigues; then march to the theatre where the rare phenomenon will take place, something which occurs only once every seventy-five years.

Company commander to lieutenant:

By order of the colonel in fatigues at 2000 hours tomorrow evening, the phenomenal Halley's Comet will appear in the theatre. In case of rain in the battalion area, the colonel will give another order, something which occurs only once every seventy-five years.

Lieutenant to sergeant:

Tomorrow at 2000 hours, the colonel, in fatigues, will appear in the theatre with Halley's Comet, something which happens every seventy-five years. If it rains, the colonel will order the comet into the battalion area.

Sergeant to the squad:

When it rains tomorrow at 2000 hours, the phenomenal seventy-five year old General Halley, accompanied by the colonel, will drive his Comet through the battalion area theatre in fatigues.

A humorous look at ourselves but one which makes the point for teaching the same things to everyone! The big question however, is at what point does duplication actually take place? The widely accepted, and taught, viewpoint is that when you sponsor someone else you have duplicated yourself.

But when you sponsor someone you have done something they haven't done, sponsor someone. Right?

Then duplication must take place when they sponsor someone, then they have duplicated you. Not so... because now you've sponsored someone and taught them to sponsor someone too. Now when the third person down from you sponsors someone, you are beginning to reach the duplication principle. Because the person you sponsor now has sponsored someone, who has sponsored someone who sponsored someone.

The principle of teaching teachers to teach teachers to teach is one that involves this same concept of duplication. Not only do we have to sponsor and duplicate ourselves, we must fulfill the full duplication principle by teaching teachers to teach teachers to teach.

The concept is not a simple one because it involves the teaching of teachers. I once saw the teaching concept demonstrated by a speaker who did not smoke. He asked for a volunteer from the audience who did. He asked the person if he could teach him to smoke. The man said he thought he could.

The speaker revealed two packs of unopened cigarettes and asked the man to begin the teaching process. The man told the speaker to put a cigarette in his mouth. The speaker stuck the whole pack in his mouth. The man said no, no, open the pack first. The speaker tore the pack to shreds and with it demolished the cigarettes inside. It was obvious that the speaker was prepared for this lesson as he picked up the second pack.

The man doing the teaching now showed the speaker carefully how to open the pack, remove the cigarette, and asked him to now put one in his mouth. The speaker placed the non-filtered end into his mouth. The more the man tried to teach, the more the man learned from his inept student!

This illustration may seem ridiculous to you, but I can't tell you how many times I have tried to teach an audience simple paperwork, and have someone ask me if the line on an application or order form which said "Social Security Number" meant "their" number? Now how silly is that? I usually respond with, "No it means to put your neighbor's number on the application!" (It's hard to resist being a smart-alec sometimes.)

Leadership and advanced training programs are meant to bring together all of the "teachers" in one place so that they are getting the story straight from the source. This will bring the core teachers back to center, back to middle C.

Throughout this book I am pointing out the function of functions (Events). Nothing is more important however than this centering process! The confused mind says no.

I once went to a training held by one of the industry's largest companies. Five of their top achievers were to speak, and I was excited and honored to be invited to close the meeting. I went early and took my note pad. The first speaker got up and told us how he had achieved his lofty status and I was impressed both by his delivery and the content.

The second speaker was just as good, but he told us something that, although not extremely different, it was significant enough to be confusing. The third speaker was a lady and she was dynamite! I was very impressed with her presentation and took many notes. The fourth and fifth speakers each had something different to offer and I took notes.

Since I have been in the industry for over twenty years, I have learned to discern between black and white issues and shades of grey. I've learned to distinguish between "core" building issues, and "peripheral" issues.

The neophytes in the room are not nearly as able to make out the differences. I must have heard two dozen people say on the way out that they would never come back again, because come Monday they were so confused that they didn't know what to do.

I see would be leaders allow new people into leadership meetings when they have not even learned to teach the basics well. The reality check is too much, and then they wonder why potentially outstanding leaders quit. They quit because they got too much too soon, or because the information was simply too confusing or devastating to handle.

Saying the business is tough is one thing, but admitting to a newcomer how much strain it can put on one's pocketbook or marriage may be too much too soon.

On the other hand, once someone has found out how tough it can be, it's time for a leadership meeting to deal with how to go forward positively in a negative environment.

Certainly some quit because they get too little information as well. The key is to learn to dole out training in measured doses.

The Master Teacher himself took three years, day and night, to teach twelve men how to lead and deal with the challenges associated with masses. It will take some time to "teach teachers to teach teachers to teach."

Chapter 15

SETTING YOUR POSTURE

"Let him who wants to move and convince others be first moved and convinced himself." -- Thomas Carlyle

At my first Diamond Club, (A designation my company used to denote a company paid award event) held at the Sonesta Beach hotel in Key Biscayne, Florida, my upline Diamond asked me, "Who do you have in your group back home who could take your business from where it is and make it grow?" I naively rose to the bait, "Well let's see there's Darrell, Kenny, and Bob." He laughed and said, "Very well, I'll ask you the same question next year." He knew something I hadn't discovered yet, and that is everything is not always as it seems.

The future of network marketing has never been brighter. Several experts place the number of participants at over twenty-two million worldwide! There are over two thousand network marketing companies selling everything from soap to telephone service. Take a number and off you go.

Before you go too far though, sit down and think about what it is going to take to do this successfully. What kind of people will be in your organization and how will you find them? What are you going to do with them once you have them? What are the pitfalls? Is there something missing in your upline, company, or product line? How about training? Who does it? What is the culture of the company? Is there a mission statement? How is the growth pattern currently?

How about vision? Have the owners been there before? In a rapidly growing business, the owners may have to reinvest more than their previous months profits! Many times this number grows exponentially, so the financial condition of the company may be an important element. What kind of computer system do they use? Have the bonus checks been paid on time? Are any top level distributors defecting? If so... Why? These questions are important to consider when you are investing your credibility, time, and money!

Network marketing is a complex web of personalities and relationships. The opportunities are immense and the frustrations many, but the road is one worth taking. It will be a long journey and one that will stretch you to your limit. Why? Because everyone is different, we are all simple in ways, and complex in other ways.

Many questions have perplexed me for years, such as; how can someone be confident and fearful? (At the same time?) How can people who dedicated themselves totally just last week quit this week? Why do you have to explain over and over again to some people? Especially something you understood before anyone explained it to you?

Why can't people make a simple phone call and invite a friend to a meeting? And get them to come? What does it take to get someone to realize that it takes time and effort to

have a larger than average income? What gets into people?
Do they think that you took them to raise? Must you do
everything for them? Can't they at least listen to the tape
and read the distributor manual?

You see what I mean? People! Just people, like you
and me, at times excited, fearful, confident, and looking for
some answers to some of life's questions.

Network marketing is a microcosm of life itself. We all
inhabit a planet that offers us nothing but opportunity. Those
of us in network marketing enjoy a freedom few in this world
get to exercise. We have the freedom to say yes or no to
our dreams. There are still some countries where a big
dream is to have three meals a day, a job to go to, a bank
account to put money into, and a tape recorder to listen to a
motivational tape or beautiful music.

And yet the average distributor in network marketing
takes their opportunity lightly. Most refuse to do what any
other businessman or woman, in any other type of business,
would take for granted.

It would be silly to try running a restaurant by opening
one night a week (Opportunity meetings). Start a print shop
and open one Saturday a month (Trainings and Events). Be
successful in your law or medical practice and never spend
time updating and improving your skills (Events).

My upline admonished that to have a million dollar
income one must treat their business as if it were already a
million dollar business. Nickel and dime your business,
procrastinate, spread doubt (Let alone negative) and your
business will surely flounder and fail.

The reason so many of your downline take the business lightly is because they have been programmed that the business is "easy" or that it "won't require much of your time," or that "the products sell themselves."

All of these are "come on" positioning statements that are designed to get new members in the "back door." The result is to create a low expectancy of work in exchange for a high expectancy of reward. In other words, when you create "something for nothing" expectancy, you usually reap what you have sown. Nothing!

Contrast the above statement of position with one where the individual is taught to recruit by selling the benefits of a successful business, and follows that with a question such as "What would you be willing to do for financial independence?"

By doing this you have given the prospect a new perspective, one you can focus on performance and commitment! Pushing the first member is like trying to push a rope. The second member will be easier to lead and more likely to stay with you through normal start-up stutter-steps than the one who thinks there will be no challenges involved. Perhaps you should program new members for toughness in advance? Vaccinate them against negative, and create a strong sense of urgency in the beginning!

The commission on someone who gets in, but doesn't do anything, is the same as on the one who didn't get in. There is a negative to sponsoring non-performers and that is that they create a false impression that the "business doesn't work." Non-performers also can slow the pack down.

I can't tell you how many times I run into people who

tell me; "Oh I tried that deal but it didn't work." When I question them further they admit that they didn't go to meetings and events, didn't really use the products, and generally didn't give the business a realistic chance to succeed.

Why is it that the non-performers are almost always the most vocal? Negative spreads faster and further than positive. I tell people who attend my seminars that the day they are truly in their respective business is the day they tear up a new member's application and check and tell them that they're not ready for the business.

I was signing a person up once who had already filled out the application and given me a check when he asked me, "Now what if I want to quit?" I tore the paperwork up, including his check, and told him I didn't think he was ready for an opportunity as good as the one I had just offered him. He was shocked, but I didn't then, and don't now, have time for those who are thinking about quitting more than they are about achievement.

Take enough pride in yourself and your business to seek out those who really want to change their lives. It will change yours in the process.

This process is known as "Setting your posture." It is a way of looking, thinking and acting. It involves everything from the way we dress to the way we walk and talk! There is a right way and a wrong way to present the products and bonus plan. There is a difference in the response of prospective new members when there exists a boldness and determination in your voice and actions.

It is true that "Man is more convinced by the depth of

your conviction than the height of your logic!"

The who's who of network marketing is not made of those who quit, or those who whine, or those who see the glass half empty! It is made of winners, who walk, talk, and eat like giants! It takes a giant attitude, a giant appetite, and a giant heart to be patient and kind and yet firm and determined. If you are to make the roll call of heroes, then you must discover the greatness of spirit that exists in you.

The following poem has always meant a lot to me and I read it daily for over a year to remind me that the "spirit itself is not always willing." The will to win relies entirely on "want." The most important element in success is desire! I suggest copying this poem and carrying it with you everywhere until you know it by heart. I hope its inspiring words will do for you what it has done for me and other seekers.

When the little things get in the way, when mowing the lawn is more important than making a few more phone calls, when cleaning house or doing laundry takes the place of reading a good positive thinking book, then you have given in to the same things everyone else does.

Take the high road. Get somebody to clean the house, do the laundry and mow the lawn. Most leaders are buried in the grave of a follower. Too bad. Most people's epitaph could be "Killed by life... one day at a time."

THE WILL TO WIN

If you want a thing bad enough

To go out and fight for it,

Work day and night for it,

Give up your time and your peace and your sleep for it.

If only desire of it

Makes you quite mad enough

Never to tire of it,

Makes you hold all other things tawdry and cheap for it,

If gladly you'll sweat for it,

Fret for it, Plan for it,

Lose all your terror of God or man for it,

If you'll simply go after that thing that you want,

With all your capacity,

Strength and sagacity,

Faith and hope and confidence, stern pertinacity,

If neither cold poverty, famished and gaunt,

Nor sickness nor pain

Of body and brain

Can turn you away from the thing that you want,

If dogged and grim you besiege and beset it,

You'll get it!

-- Berton Braley

Chapter 16

RUNNING TO WIN!

"You can't cross the sea merely by standing and staring at the water." -- Rabindranath Tagore

In "Raising a Giant," I related a story of my cousin who never bought property when we played the game of Monopoly. Her rationale was that even though she didn't win, she got to play longer. Many people today, go about life in much the same way. They can't win because they aren't even in the race!

There is much said today about what it takes to be a winner in the network marketing race. Certain things are constants and must be done to assure you and your downline of continued success. I have seen many formulas but none as powerful as the one that follows.

To be successful at network marketing you and your downline must do four things.

I. Remove Distractions

This may mean putting aside golf, bowling, fishing or something you enjoy doing for a short time. It may mean resigning from a committee to make time for the business, or hiring a maid to clean the house, or a neighborhood kid to mow your lawn while you build your business. In most of our busy lives something has to go so that we can elevate our priorities to a new level.

The thing all us of have to deal with is the draw that everyday life has on our downline. Let's face it, when you have kids, it is Little League today and ballet tomorrow. Little Janie has the flu and Bobby has an ear infection. See what I mean? Life.

If it's not bowling leagues, parent teacher meetings, and summer league softball, then there's church and civic activities, the movies, concerts and don't forget favorite television programs… can anyone say "Internet Time?"

All of these are distractions that a real network marketer must deal with, not only in your own life, but in the lives of each member in the downline!

When I first signed up in network marketing, I was on the board of directors of the local Rotary Club, the Building Committee of my church, was Music and Youth Director at my church, taught the biggest Sunday School class at my church, and had a wife and five kids.

My insurance business took up a good deal of my time and I had enrolled in a CLU class to advance my career in insurance. Talk about busy!

My life was not too unlike those of the winners in your business today. I had to come to the realization that if I kept my network marketing career in the low priority position it was in I was not going to be a success!

Something had to go. The truth is, my life had gotten

out of control. I didn't have a good handle on priorities.
Sound familiar?

II. Remember why you are doing this

So many of us get caught up in the negatives in life
that we lose sight of the real important things. Consider all
of the good things that could happen to you and your family
if you had more income. Would you buy that dream house?
Add on to your present one? Have a swimming pool built in
your backyard? How about a new car? A dream vacation to
Disney World with your children? College tuition? A new
sailboat? Or better yet, how about retiring from your job and
being in network marketing full time?

It's easy to lose sight of why we are doing this.
Keeping focused on why will cause the little things that get in
the way and cause pain to seem smaller and insignificant in
the total picture. It's the old "When you're up to your keesters
in alligators, it's hard to remember that the objective was to
drain the swamp."

Pictures and posters remind us daily of the visible
things that will come to us if we focus on the outcome and
commit to the process. The biggest killer in network
marketing is discouragement and keeping a happy heart will
assure us of a first line defense against discouragement.
Pick something that symbolizes to you the ultimate in life.
Something that's easy to see in your mind when you close
your eyes and think about it.

In the chapter on "Living the Dream," you will find my
admonishments to demonstrate to your group why you are
involved. Don't drift away; stay focused, and you will find the

business much easier to do and you too will be a happy warrior.

III. Resist discouragement

The biggest killer of dreams is discouragement. One thing all winners have in common is how they handle discouragement. Most of us think that the winners have fewer problems. The fact is they have as much or more than anyone. They just choose to deal with them on a more positive note. Discouragement visits every home and everyone every day. It is a fact of life.

Listen to CDs and DVDs, read positive thinking books, associate with those people who lift you up instead of those who bring you down. Run with the big dogs; leave the puppy chow to those who never grew up. This is a big business for big thinkers with big dreams. (Special note: Sometimes little thinkers become big thinkers.)

To become a giant you must rise above defeat and pettiness. It is about taking on the look and feel of a positive leader. It is about going to the well and coming away filled. It is about being a reservoir so that those who come to you for filling can be filled.

Wouldn't it be great to have people say of you that "every word and deed lifted others up?" You can be that kind of person. It begins with reading, listening to CDs and DVDs, and plugging into those who are themselves "Leader Feeders."

Not only do our children look to us to set the example, so does our downline, and in no other area is our failure more obvious than when we allow ourselves to fall prey to discouragement. It just isn't done!

IV. Rely upon the system

Don't reinvent the wheel. Millions of people everyday stray from the proven path into the bar ditch of failure. They ignore the principles of success and expect good results. Don't be one of these.

Sure, there are those who have made it big in network marketing because of good luck, or some magic tape, or "heal you in a minute" scheme; but they ultimately fall by the wayside because their methods are not duplicatable or repeatable. (Very often they're not even respectable.)

The old adage, the harder I work the luckier I get is a good one. There is a "System" that works. It is learnable, teachable, and doable for anyone. Far better to rely on "The System" than to expect the lottery to bring us our goals and dreams. Get plugged into events. Set your goal to reach the next level of achievement with your company. Let others know what your goal is. Set the pace.

As you will see in later chapters, the need for a duplicatable and uniform system is vital. No organization can survive for long if there isn't a support system. The reason may not be obvious to you, but you will soon learn the limits of one person's one-to-one ability.

This means there must be a way to create a group support system that people understand, get motivated by and find rewarding.

In your absence the show must go on. In the absence of your mentor or upline leaders, the business must continue unimpeded; you are totally reliant on this system. Without it, you will be like General Custer at the Little Big Horn, outnumbered and out manned.

Chapter 17

THE GREAT, THE LONELY, & THE DEAD

"Nothing is more powerful than an idea whose time has come." -- Anonymous

In 1981, I had reached the pinnacle of my initial success in network marketing. I was beginning to experience the first serious pains of leadership. My business had grown unrestricted for five years. They had been halcyon years. Now a new era was beginning, one I was totally unprepared for, but did not know or believe that. I was full of myself and believed that I could handle any situation that confronted me. (Proving once again the ignorance of false confidence.)

What I didn't know however, would soon destroy my finely tuned machine. Like a fine race car speeding around the track with a slight motor oil leak, my enormously successful organization was coming apart at the seams. Someone once said that "what you don't know won't hurt you," but I'm here to tell you that what you don't know, that you don't know, will hurt you. I was like a blind man in a dark room looking for a black cat that wasn't there.

There is a new breed of "Third Wave" high tech network marketers who are nothing more than glorified

153

stamp lickers. Their network marketing experience is limited to buying a mailing list and sending out CDs and DVDs. They haven't the slightest idea how to connect with and lead a large downline of people.

I have been accused of being "old fashioned" and "out of touch with the times." If that means ignoring people, making them feel like a number on someone's broadcast fax machine, then I plead guilty!

Making people feel important and developing leadership skills, building dreams and hopes, is what the industry I know and love is about! I believe in leaders! Strong, compassionate, intelligent, and visionary leaders. People who build on a solid foundation for the future and are broken hearted when they let those they lead down.

I've spent more than my share of sleepless nights because I could not forget that I let someone down who was counting on me. Still, there are many who believed and followed me and today, are better because of some small contribution I made to their success. I take some pride in knowing that in a small way I was able to impact the lives of a few.

In October of 1981 I was doing an in home meeting for a pharmacist in the Oklahoma City area. I met a man and his wife we'll just refer to them as Bob and June. Bob, too, was a pharmacist, and at the conclusion of the meeting told me he wasn't interested in the program.

More than that, he said he was happy being a "small town druggist." He related how tough he found it to talk to people, and how he could not imagine himself selling anything.

I told Bob that he "was dead" and that "his friends just didn't have the courage to bury him." I figured I'd never see him again after that. Instead, he and June showed up the next week with another couple in tow, got into the business and started coming to meetings.

I had a potluck dinner for the group a few weeks later and asked each person to tell the group why they were in the business. When it came Bob's turn, he rose with sweat dripping off his red face, and he said, "A few weeks ago, this man, he pointed to me, said I was dead." He continued, "Worse than that he said I was dull," (I'd forgotten I said that.) Bob said, "The reason I'm in the business is because I had quit on life. I'd lost my dreams. My dream is to one day earn the right to stand on a stage with 10,000 people in the audience and tell them how I overcame my weaknesses and how they can too."

I was floored! I didn't see Bob and June after I sold my business. I heard they'd moved on to another network marketing company and were doing well. Then one day a letter came. It simply said, "Thanks for all you have done. Last night I spoke to 14,000 people for over an hour, and can you believe it, they gave me a standing ovation?" Yes, Bob, I can believe it!

Congratulations to the entire Bob's" of the world who have found the courage to step out of their comfort zone and into the uncertain light of leadership! I take great pride in the small role I played in Bob's life. Someday you too will take courage in the fact you helped someone awaken from a lifelong slumber, into the light of a new and exciting future.

NEWSWEEK MAGAZINE

Newsweek magazine ran the following column only a few days before the inauguration of President Ronald Reagan. I clipped it out and have read it often in the years since then. I hope you will keep these observations in mind as you build your castle of dreams.

"At a moment when we are waiting to see whether we have elected a President or a leader, it is worth examining the differences between the two. For not every President is a leader, but every time we elect a President we hope for one, especially in times of doubt and crisis. In easy times we are ambivalent - the leader, after all, makes demands, challenges the status quo, and shakes things up.

Leadership is as much a question of timing as anything else. The leader must appear on the scene at a moment when people are looking for leadership, as Churchill did in 1940, as Roosevelt did in 1993, as Lenin did in 1917. And when he comes, he must offer a simple, eloquent message.

Great leaders are almost always great simplifiers, who cut through argument, debate and doubt to offer a solution everybody can understand and remember. Churchill warned the British to expect Blood, toil, tears and sweat: FDR told Americans that the only thing we have to fear is fear itself: Lenin promised the war-weary Russians peace, land and bread. Straightforward but potent messages.

We have an image of what a leader ought to be. We even recognize the physical signs: leaders may not necessarily be tall, but they must have bigger-than-life, commanding features such as LBJ's nose and ear lobes,

Ike's broad grin. A trademark also comes in handy: Lincoln's stovepipe hat, JFK's rocker. We expect our leaders to stand out a little, not to be like ordinary men. Half of President Ford's trouble lay in the fact that if you closed your eyes for a moment, you couldn't remember his face, figure or clothes. A leader should have an unforgettable identity, instantly and permanently fixed in people's minds.

Special: It also helps for a leader to be able to do something most of us cannot: FDR overcame polio; Mao swam the Yangtze River at the age of 72. We don't want our leaders to be Just like us we want them to be like us, but better, special, more so. Yet if they are too different, we reject them. Adlai Stevenson was too cerebral… Nelson Rockefeller… too rich.

Even television, which comes in for a lot of knocks as an image-builder that magnifies form over substance, doesn't altogether obscure the qualities of leadership we recognize, or their absence. Television exposed Nixon's insecurity, Humphrey's fatal infatuation with his own voice.

A leader must know how to use power (that's what leadership is about), but he also has to have a way of showing that he does. He has to be able to project firmness- no physical clumsiness (like Ford), no rapid eye movements (like Carter).

A Chinese philosopher once remarked that a leader must have the grace of a good dancer, and there is a great deal of wisdom to this. A leader should know how to appear relaxed and confident. His walk should be firm and purposeful. He should be able, like Lincoln, FDR, Truman, Ike and JFK to give a good, hearty, belly laugh, instead of the sickly grin that passes for good humor in Nixon or Carter.

Ronald Reagan's training as an actor showed to good effect in the debate with Carter, when by his easy manner and apparent affability, he managed to convey the impression that in fact he was the President and Carter the challenger.

If we know what we're looking for, why is it so difficult to find? The answer lies in a very simple truth about leadership. People can only be led where they want to go. The leader follows, though a step ahead. Americans wanted to climb out of the Depression and needed someone to tell them they could do it, and FDR did. The British believed that they could still win the war after the defeats of 1940, and Churchill told them they were right.

A leader rides the waves, moves with the tides, understands the deepest yearnings of his people. He cannot make a nation that wants peace at any price go to war, or stop a nation determined to fight from doing so. His purpose must match the national mood. His task is to focus the people's energies and desires, to define them in simple terms, to inspire, to make what people already want seem attainable, important, within their grasp.

Above all, he must dignify our desires, convince us that we are taking part in the making of great history, and give us a sense of glory about ourselves. Winston Churchill managed, by sheer rhetoric, to turn the British defeat and the evacuation of Dunkirk in 1940 into a major victory. FDR's words turned the sinking of the American fleet at Pearl Harbor into a national rallying cry instead of a humiliating national scandal. A leader must stir our blood, not appeal to our reason.

Fallacy: For this reason, businessmen generally make poor leaders. They tend to be pragmatists who think that once you've explained why something makes sense, people will do it; but history shows the fallacy of this belief. When times get tough, people don't want to be told what went wrong, or lectured, or given a lot of complicated statistics and plans (like Carter's energy policy) they don't understand. They want to be moved, excited, inspired, consoled, uplifted - in short, led!

A great leader must have a certain irrational quality, a stubborn refusal to face facts, infectious optimism, and the ability to convince us that all is not lost even when we're afraid it is. Confucius suggested that, while the advisers of a great leader should be as cold as ice, the leader himself should have fire, a spark of divine madness.

He won't come until we're ready for him, for the leader is like a mirror, reflecting back to us our own sense of purpose, putting into words our own dreams and hopes, transforming our needs and fears into coherent policies and programs.

Our strength makes him strong: our determination makes him determined; our courage makes him a hero; he is, in the final analysis, the symbol of the best in us, shaped by our own spirit and will. And when these qualities are lacking in us, we cannot produce him, and even with all our skill at image building, we cannot fake him. He is, after all, merely the sum of us."

What characteristics do you admire the most in a good leader? Is it someone who is strong and a great visionary / protector? Or do you go for a quieter type? Someone who leads from behind rather than out front?

There are many lessons to be learned about

leadership and the greatest one may be that leaders come in all sizes, shapes, and descriptions. Some are gregarious and bombastic, some are quiet and somber. There isn't a mold or one model that works. In network marketing, you will encounter them all.

The strong leader must at times be soft and caring. The quiet leader must at times get in someone's face and stand their ground. Leaders must not be weak, but they must at times be vulnerable. They are not allowed to show fear or uncertainty. The leader must lead by example, teach, and excite. Be a visionary, and build alliances with other key leaders.

I wish I had known then what I know now. I would talk less and listen more. I would watch my alliances and remember who the true friends were. I can never change what happened, or mend the lives that were hurt by my ignorance. What I can do is shine light on the truth as I have experienced it first hand, so that you do not have to go down that long and winding, heartbreaking road.

Chapter 18

THE FELLOWSHIP OF FOLLOWSHIP

"No matter how smart I am, my group does what I do, not what I say." -- Crisp's Law #1

The temptation to write abstractly is always there in my business. This chapter will take you into some specific areas where I feel the rubber meets the road. New leaders sometimes have a problem determining their "style," and finding the harmony of leadership. I have stated before that network marketing is 60 – 70 percent art form and 30 - 40 percent science.

The "Art" of building a network marketing business is just as teachable as the "Science" it's just that it takes more dedication to learn the art.

This chapter will set you on a course toward learning why people perform. Have you ever asked yourself why some football coaches get more out of their players than others?   Why do some churches grow, while others are stagnant and have been the same for years? Don't all coaches have access to players and know the rules of the game? Aren't all preachers privy to the scriptures? If so, then why are the results so different?

It has always fascinated me that people study every aspect of building a successful downline, except the one I feel is most important.

Here are five key points which will help you to remember the key elements in successful network building. It is widely agreed that man is a "creature of fellowship." People love to do things with other people. (They even love to fail with others.) Look at the people who get tattoos. Rarely do they ever go by themselves. No. Instead, they'll talk a friend into going and defacing their bodies too.

People learn negative habits from other people. No one sits alone and decides to do drugs or become abusive. Instead, doing drugs and learning abusive behavior are habits most often picked up from a friend or relative. Good students rarely run with poor students. Athletes hang out with athletes. Artists tend to associate with other artists.

Most bad habits stem from bad experiences. Man is a creature of fellowship, and learns much of what he learns from his environment. Therefore, it is your responsibility to take on the role of "new habit maker."

To become a new habit maker you must do five things.

I. Feature it!

Try to "see it" before anyone else does. There are two types of sight ... Eyesight and Insight! Most people only see things with their eyes, after the fact or event has become a reality. Real leaders see the facts in their minds before they happen, and have a knack for getting others to see the vision too.

Visualization is the mother of all good things. Napoleon Hill, the father of all modern success philosophy, and the author of the bestselling book "Think and Grow

Rich," said the beginning of all good things is in "Creative Thinking." A good leader spends hours just thinking about how they can do things today and tomorrow with the group that will cause them to visualize the future in a brighter and more dynamic way.

Hill also said that "Imagination is one of the keys to success." He taught that "Wherever the spirit of teamwork is the domination influence in business or industry -- success is inevitable."

Perhaps you remember the story Hill liked to tell of Edwin C. Barnes who worked with the great inventor Thomas Edison. Barnes was telling a friend one day how he was making $12,000 a year working for Edison. The friend replied "You're a partner of the great Edison, but making only $12,000 a year? Why, if I had your opportunity, I'd be making ten times that amount!" This was not exactly the reply he had hoped to get, but when the shock wore off, he asked his friend how?

His friend said, "I'll tell you how! You're engaged in selling the Edison Dictating Machine and you naturally have a force of salesmen in the field. I would form a friendly alliance with the salesman of other related products, those who sell filing cabinets, calculators, cash registers, and office materials and exchange information about whose expanding and might be prospects for each other's merchandise. This sort of teamwork would cost no one anything but the time required to write down the names on cards and hand them in -- but it would provide both groups with high quality sales leads."

The results, according to Hill's account, were immediate and encouraging. Mr. Barnes income leaped far beyond the "ten times" increase his friend had promised. Fellowship or teamwork is necessary to assure the success of any endeavor, especially network marketing.

II. Feel It!

Nothing happens until someone gets uncomfortable! The mother eagle stirs up her nest to get the young eagles to try their wings. Most people drift through life allowing others to determine their moods and desires. Limitations are emphasized more than opportunities.

Those that succeed in network marketing do so because they are convinced beyond any doubt that there's is the best opportunity on the planet. Being unreasonable where this is concerned is a good idea.

Develop a powerful sense of purpose. My sponsor challenged me to "burn" to "catch on fire!" Most of us react emotionally to daily life. Unfortunately, most of what happens pushes us into a dark hole and into depression. You cannot allow this to happen to you! You cannot allow this to happen to your teammates!

People buy in to their circumstances perpetuating past negative results. Subscribe to the old adage, "It's better to act your way into a new way of feeling, than to feel your way into a new way of acting."

A close relative turned down my offers to sponsor him into my first network marketing endeavor. His reason? "I don't think I would like doing it." My response was, "That's not required." Most people go to jobs they don't like everyday... They wear clothes that don't lift their spirits.

Drive cars that don't make them proud, and live in homes beneath their heritage as winners.

Feeling down is not a requirement to live on this planet! You're entitled to feel up, empowered, and happy! Stop giving permission to the doomsday crowd to put you down. You were born to win, to succeed, to lead others and to live on the mountain top with other high achievers!

III. Fight for it!

Life is war! Someone once offered this simple advice, "In the war of life… **FIGHT BACK**!" Don't just fight, but fight the good fight and don't give up. Let yourself get excited more than ever before. People are moved by those who feel the tides and harmonies of life and let themselves get caught up in the moment. Be passionate, it's your life! If you can't get excited about your success, then there isn't anyone in this world excited about it!

The book of Psalms (23) encourages us with these empowering words, "I will fear no evil." We are living under constant attack! Our intellect is under attack! Our enthusiasm is under attack! Our energy is under attack! And our attitude is under attack! Jim Rohn reminds us in his book "The Four Seasons" that in this life, "All good things will be attacked and every garden will be invaded!"

I have always been inspired by the actions of those in American history that have had the spirit of the great patriot John Paul Jones. You may remember that it was he who uttered the famous words, "I have only yet begun to fight." (My son thinks it was Evandor Hollyfield) We have a great heritage of winning. Tap into the idea that those who "fight on," emerge victorious in the end.

Bear Bryant said that "A man who won't be beat, can't be beat." If you want real success, then the challenge for you and your downline is going to be to rise to the occasion and fight against lethargy, negative attacks from the outside, and fear itself! It was the same legendary coach who put a sign up over the Crimson Tide's locker room door which simply read "Be good, or be gone!"

A member of the USA ski team was asked if she were not afraid of getting hurt? She replied, "I'm more afraid of being nothing than I am of being hurt." "Fight on" should be the battle cry. At the height of the German bombardment of London Winston Churchill said, "They'll find me in the last trench!"

Dreams born in the heart and mind, cannot die of circumstances, they can only die in the heart and mind. Don't let anyone steal your dreams!

IV. Find it and enjoy it!

We reach outward destinations through an inward journey. Life should be a celebration. But how can we enjoy fighting? If we are under constant attack, then how can we celebrate? The answer is simple. When you are on the journey toward your dreams, then the road itself becomes your "Highway to heaven." You can always have a happy warrior's heart. This will amaze your fellow travelers and annoy your enemies.

The challenge is the reward itself. Most people get up every morning and go to a job that is boring and unfulfilling. They have a business that runs them. For many, life has become either a rat race, or a pathetic pathway to nowhere.

I've heard people say, "I'm going to do this even if it kills me." Well I appreciate the dedication, but with that attitude, it likely will kill you before you reach your destination.

I met a young lady named Cherisse one day while shopping. She was well dressed and vibrant! She walked right up to me, stuck out her hand and introduced herself, complemented me, and asked if I would be interested in a business opportunity? I was impressed with her boldness. I said," I might be what have you got?" She replied, with a huge smile, "I don't have the time to tell you the details today, but if you have a business card I'll call for an appointment."

I quickly discovered that Cherisse was involved in a network marketing company, and that she had been involved for about a year. I asked her how it was going and she said, "very well, thank you." I asked how many she had in her downline, she said, "fifty or so." I asked, "How many were active?" She bowed her head and said, "only about five or six," she quickly perked back up again and said with great enthusiasm, that she had never been more excited about anything in her life than she was about her company, and her prospects for success.

Now here's a young lady that was not making a significant amount of money, nor has she set the world of network marketing on fire, but she is a success. Why? Because she has a happy heart! She is enjoying the journey! I met Cherisse two years ago and lost touch with her. I ran into her again just recently, and you know she is still at it, still excited, and still sharing her love of her business with anyone who will listen.

The greatest lie ever told... "When I get everything I want, then I'll be happy."

V. *Don't forget it!*

Losing sight of the goal causes us to lose heart. Burn your dreams and goals indelibly in your mind. Share them only with those who will reinforce them, and keep them from those who would belittle you or put you down. Napoleon Hill challenged his students to find people who share your vision. He called this group a "Mastermind." You can use their encouragement and advice to push you toward your objectives.

Remember that even though you are by yourself, that you're not alone! This is a terrific lesson. Every night when I started my car to go out and share the business with someone, I reminded myself that at approximately at the same hour, there were thousands of other seekers starting their cars and heading out to fight the fight too! If they can do it you can do it.

The Good Book says that "as we go, our faith will increase." The going is the knowing! Dead men don't bleed! You're alive with a dream worthy of your very best. Don't forget it and don't let anyone steal the joy of going for it from you!

If it ain't worth fighting for, it ain't worth having!

Dr. Robert Schuller admonishes us not to surrender to "Faces, Forces, Farces or Fears but to keep the Faith."

Good advice! Long ago I found this quotation that simply says, "Faith is the bird that feels the light, and sings while the dawn is still dark."

I wrote these words to myself when it all seemed to be going against me, when friends turned their backs to me, and things looked the bleakest. I was staying at the Peabody hotel in Orlando, Florida and had just gotten another piece of bad news. (All do respects to Nike, I penned this long before their ads appeared on the scene)

Some say the game is over. They give up and go home. They play "not to lose" instead of to win. They sound the death knell of opportunity. They say the home team will never score, that we'll never win. They tell us to be satisfied with what we've got.

But I say the game ain't over, it's just the bottom of the first inning. Sure, their pitcher is throwing fire, but our best hitters are just coming up to the plate! The fat lady hasn't even got her dress on, the fans are still coming in and finding their seats. Hot dogs still hot, beer still cold, and the vendor isn't even sweating.

The game is young and so am I, now it's my turn to take my cuts at the ball, I get to bat again, and again. Oh sure, you can say it's over, but that's not for me. It's not my way! I'll take batting practice till my hands bleed. I'll go to the gym and get stronger! I'll go to the track and get faster! I came to win!

It ain't over until I SAY IT'S OVER!

Chapter 19

SPONSORING AND WORKING WITH PROFESSIONALS

"Anyone can be up when they're up, but a leader is up when they're down."   -- Dexter Yager

We are not all equal. Some of us are ravishingly beautiful, some are ravishingly plain. Some have knack for the physical, while others are more into emotional or spiritual things. Some people can't change a light bulb without help; others can overhaul a jet engine with a screwdriver and a pair of pliers. All of us are loved by our Creator equally, and each of us has a divine destiny of this I am sure.

I am a college dropout. Not that I am ignorant or unable to learn or study, it's just a fact that I didn't complete my college degree. I admire those who did without putting down those who didn't (Including Me). I have however, experienced the joy of working with professional people. Not that all professionals are fun to work with, it is just that I have discovered that working with people who have a well developed network, starting out, is easier than those who do not.

170

I have also discovered that one of the keys to building a successful network marketing business is to find people who understand the concept of "delayed gratification." Most professionals have spent years in training themselves for a high income occupation. These years were usually years of struggle and hard work for little or no pay. Investing a few hours each week, for a potential income that is greater than the one they went to school for eight years to attain, is nothing.

In four years I built an organization of two hundred thousand people. It didn't happen by accident. There were some very important factors that led to this. One of the key elements in that phenomenal growth... professionals, several thousand of them!

The years were 1975 - 1980 and things were a mess in the U.S. economy. Interest rates were pushing 20% and unemployment was at an all time high. The company I was with had stalled out at around two hundred million in annual sales. The general impression was that the company had "topped out." Many thought that "saturation" had finally gotten to them. There "simply weren't enough people left to sponsor, for anyone to succeed anymore!"

To compound the problem, I lived in a state where, according to those who had tried before, "It couldn't be done." So what's a man to do when things look so bleak? Go for it I say!

In the depression of the twenties when everyone was selling, one man was buying, that man was named J. Paul Getty. When everyone is getting out, may be the very time for you to get in!

I started very slowly. My sixth month bonus check was a mere $3.63. Not a dynamite beginning by anyone's standards. My sponsor convinced me to go to a meeting in Ashville, North Carolina called a Family Reunion. It was at this meeting that I met my first network marketing millionaire, Rick Setzer. This guy was slicker than a red sled!

When I first saw him I couldn't believe my eyes. He was wearing the prettiest pair of red Sansabelt golf slacks I ever saw! He had on a pair of white patent leather boots and a gaudy golf shirt... in short he was my kind of guy!

Rick was talking to a couple of school teachers from a small town nearby. He pulled out a wad of money that would have choked an elephant. I was impressed.

First impressions notwithstanding, Rick Setzer and I became great friends. Rick taught me a lot about people and dreaming big dreams. It was Rick that taught me how to nurture and bring along leaders. It was Rick that encouraged me when I was having difficulty getting my people to fall into line. It was Rick who soothed the downline wounds that I opened up.

Probably one of the best pieces of advice Rick ever gave me was "It's hard to work with broke people." Broke people, he explained, make "broke people" decisions. They generally don't understand the difference between "invest" and "spend" (As in "You did what with the rent money?") "You spent the rent money on CDs and DVDs?"

This advice and the fact that I found out early in my business that professionals usually had a larger network than non-professionals. I discovered that professionals usually carry more influence than do non-professionals.

As I said earlier, I do not have a college degree and no one ever referred to me as a "Professional" before I wrote books. I have met many people who began in network marketing nearly penniless, and became millionaires. I am always looking for the next pop truck driver, waitress, or beer truck driver who wants to do something else with their life. But the fact is that someone has to buy products for anyone to get paid. This means money.

If people who can't afford products sponsor people who can't afford them either, then the cycle of "broke" never ends. No company pays commission on products that haven't been purchased. (I believe that everyone who WANTS TO can find a way)

In assessing the general population, one quickly realizes that there are more broke people than any other kind. This means that all of us will be working with those whose previous efforts have moved them all the way along to a stressed out financial condition. However, this fact does not mean that we should not seek to sponsor higher income professionals. (Along with our efforts to sponsor our share of the broke ones too)

Let's take a closer look at why these professionals would be interested in doing network marketing.

Network marketing is a form of "backup insurance" for some. For others, it may be a form of "income diversification," or an "exit strategy" for an occupation which is filled with tension and high pressure.

People in the medical community are notoriously bad investors. They usually live above their means which means they're broke at a different level than most. (You'll probably agree that it's better to be broke at two hundred thousand a year than broke at twenty-five thousand!) I like to sponsor high income people because they have a larger need level. They are accustom to working long hours and usually have well developed skills with people.

The professional usually begins with a good "warm market" list. It is important to them however, that their influence be used wisely and not abused by someone with no tact or class. I always promise that above and foremost that I would not embarrass them. Remember, the professional may be concerned that if someone finds out they are in network marketing, that this might not only reflect badly on them personally, but could make patients think that the doctor's practice is not doing well.

To a professional, prestige is an important thing. Failure in a business endeavor may reduce his/her self esteem or standing in the community. So you get a small taste of what you may be dealing with when trying to sponsor a professional or high income business owner.

Having said all that however, there are many good reasons why the professional should take a serious look at network marketing. First, it is an excellent way to back up your income. Second, it provides an exit strategy for those who are looking to "get out;" third, it is probably the only arena where you can make the kind of income the professional is accustom to, without making a substantial investment.

Professionals not only live at a different level than most, they also think on a different level. Their time is very important to them, so when you're calling or meeting with them, you should always ask, "How are we doing for time?"

Or "Am I catching you at a good time?" My best friend is a dentist and my golfing buddy. I call him at his office two or three times a week. I always ask his receptionist "Is the doctor in surgery?" I know he'll talk to me if he's not, but even for a friend, it is inconsiderate to ask someone who's at work to take time when they are busy.

When approaching a professional, you'll always want to know something about him, his practice, and family situation (Especially if he is going through a divorce or has just gone through one), how many children does he have, what does his practice or business consist of?

We know that today "managed healthcare" is hurting most people in the private sector of the medical community. It is not unusual today for a medical doctor or dentist to be earning half what they were making just a year or two ago.

Do your homework. Find out what motivates this person. Don't stumble around and present an image of someone who doesn't know what they are doing. Maybe you should enlist a more successful upline to assist in your effort to sponsor your physician or dentist. There is no harm in asking, but please give them something more to go on than "This is my doctor, can you please sponsor him for me?"

I used to do an opportunity meeting once a month that was limited to high income professional people only. (We drew the line at a minimum of one hundred thousand dollars of annual income.) The meetings were very successful.

Why separate or focus on one type of prospect? Very simple. When you talk to higher income people, the approach and focus differs from what someone in mainstream America is thinking about.

Higher income people probably are not as interested in a few hundred dollars a month as others might be. By mixing the two you run the risk of turning one or the other off.

Lower income people do not relate to the higher income person's problems. (The mechanic at the garage probably doesn't care what it costs the doctor for malpractice insurance.) What to one may be simply a matter of a zero or two, to the other is the difference in survival and starving.

The higher income person understands deferred gratification, while my brother-in-law considers waiting until Friday for his paycheck... deferred gratification.

The "meeting after the meeting" is different with the higher income person. Getting them started may also vary from the norm. I've had numerous doctors ask that no one else be allowed to come to their home for their initial meetings. Sometimes I agree with this, and at times I have another group I think is compatible, so I ask the doctor to make an exception. I have the conversation in total privacy to protect both groups. Doctors can be egotistical and aloof, and I don't want them turning off the rest of the group because of something they say or do. (Maybe that's why I get along with them so well.)

Please understand it isn't a case of "elitism" as much as it is a common sense approach to starting someone with a higher level of success, off on a good note. This may also apply to movie stars, professional athletes, high income business owners, and politicians.

Now may be a good time to add that once the

professional is "in," I treat him/her much the same as I would anyone else. No exceptions. Doctors pay to get into events, take tickets, setup chairs, hang banners, and do as much "dirty work" as anyone else. The funny thing is, in my experience, they usually complain about this less than anyone else! It is important to stress to everyone the "no favoritism" rule. (Everyone who builds is my favorite.)

You can grow faster with people of influence. It is just a fact! So what are the other considerations? I'm glad you asked. High income people are busy. It is difficult to get into their schedules. Cancellations are not uncommon. They can be babies! Their egos are fragile, but they can be fun to work with.

I personally like to work with people with big egos. They are easier to motivate and see the big picture! They don't like to be left out; therefore, they will do almost anything to be included. Once you get their attention they will be like maniacs on a mission and they will never give up. They look at it this way, "It took me nine years to go through undergraduate studies, graduate school, or medical school, plus internship and residency training added more time. So what are four or five years to become financially independent?"

What the high income professional person can do is elevate the status of your business. Those with less will look at these people and believe that because they are in the business, then it must be a good business. This will encourage them and give them confidence to "sponsor up" themselves. It's true what they say that "A rising tide lifts all ships."

You can't win the Kentucky Derby with a plow mule.

And you can't win in network marketing by sponsoring every down and out person you meet. No one enjoys a good "rags to riches" story more than I do, but I am a pragmatist when it comes to talent.

Some people can sing, and some can't, but everyone has a song in their heart. My business would not have grown as fast as it did if I had to wait for everyone to "catch up."

The first person I sponsored was a doctor, the second was a pharmacist, the third a senior systems analyst with a masters in math, the fourth an architect, the fifth a Deputy Sheriff, the sixth a life insurance agent and "Million Dollar Round Table" member, the seventh a banker, an uncle was eighth, the uncle didn't do anything but sponsor one person who was a chemical engineer who became a Diamond.

In my first five years the organization grew to the point that I had five frontline Diamond legs and twenty-nine Diamonds in the downline. Of the first twelve Diamonds all but two had advanced degrees and I was one of the two who did not.

In all, I sponsored forty-seven people on my "frontline" in nine years. Most of them had advanced degrees and their average income was around one hundred thousand dollars before they got in. Today, twenty-two years later, the business I started in my garage at 14 Choctaw Place, Claremore, Oklahoma, still does millions of dollars of business each month.

There were many success stories from my business that began with someone who barely graduated from high school. Stories like the pop truck driver who went from a

900 square foot rent house to a mansion in four years, or my best friend in high school, a Deputy Sheriff, who after four years in the business went off to seminary, and didn't work his business for five years, living solely off the income from his network marketing business.

I remember a college professor driving a ten year old Camaro up to the Howard Johnson's hotel in Tulsa for our Thursday night opportunity meeting. The windows in the doors were missing and the doors had been welded shut. Quite impressive! He quit teaching school after three years and became a millionaire in our business. His biggest leg started with a "biker," with wild hair down to the seat of his pants, and a chopped Harley for his only transportation. All great people… all fearful… hopeful… and in need of an opportunity to prove themselves.

The biker's goal was to buy a small piece of land in the country and put a trailer on it and raise a bunch of kids… and that's just what he did… a winner? You betcha.

The professionals merely added credence to it all. They made us all believe in the "worthiness" of the endeavor. Look around you and ask yourself, "Who is doing this?" You'll probably be amazed at the level of excellence that exists in the people in your company too.

Author's Note:

The purpose of this chapter is not to extol the virtues of sponsoring professionals, or those with advanced degrees. But to alert you to the fact that there is some potential that you may have missed. If you've failed to share your business with the sharpest people you know, then shame on you. I remind you however, that far more people in my group were college dropouts like me, than had advanced degrees.

Chapter 20

MANAGING – MOTIVATING - AND MOVING THE MASS

"Don't save your best, give your best."

-- Roger Blake AAM Canada

Long ago, someone told me that the key to growth in my group would be to understand that you "Manage things, and Lead People." Most people believe that you manage people and own things! Network marketing is all about treating others better than they've ever been treated before. This does not mean coddling or placating them all the time.

Sometimes the best way to treat someone is the way you would treat them if they were in a position of power or influence. Sometimes you push, sometimes you pull, and sometimes you just love them mercilessly. A good motto might be, "We're going to treat you so many ways you're bound to like one of them."

The Manager / Leader

Managing the group takes time, lots of it. The more

you can lay off these duties to your upline the better, but don't expect your upline to have new found insight if they haven't had a mentor to show them the way! This business is a chain reaction of good builder/managers teaching good builder/managers. Every good manager in this business must first demonstrate that they are good builders!

The management duties most prominently required in today's fast moving networks is one who is a manager of information and information flow. Conference calls are useless and maybe even damaging if they are not well planned and executed.

Consider in advance. Who will speak on the call? In what order? What is the call's objective? Who will be invited to listen? How long do you expect the call to run? What will it cost you and those who call in?

Events take up a lot of a good manager's time. Calling hotels and meeting facilities is a never ending job. Getting the word out of when and where the meetings will be held and coordinating with the company and upline is a major headache that often gets frustrating and results in hurt feelings and flared tempers.

I believe companies should be responsible for "overseeing" the event system, not for executing the events. The corporation should execute a national convention once a year and should stage leadership retreats, as well as one or two incentive trips. The rest is better done by field leaders.

Newsletters are many times more damaging than effective. They take up a lot of "building time" and should be relegated as the responsibility of a few. First of all, they are expensive to print and to mail. Second, one well informed upline with a part-time secretary can compile all the information essential for the group to know and send it to everyone.

Things that should NOT appear in a newsletter.

1. Names of newcomers

2. Your monthly volume

3. Telephone numbers of anyone in the group except yours

4. The number of new recruits each period

5. Income figures for distributors

6. Negative comments about others or other companies

Things that should appear in newsletters...

1. New pin winner's names

2. Dates, locations, times, and speakers at next events

3. Information regarding new programs

4. Product promotions

5. Promotion of tools such as "CD or DVD of the Week" or "Book of the Month"

6. The year ahead schedule

7. Themes and sales promotions

I've seen it all. Newsletters so sloppy that anyone paying attention would be embarrassed to have an intelligent person read one. Newsletters that welcome every newcomer thus revealing the slow growth of the entire group.

Stating your volume or income is a no-win situation, if it is large it may discourage some, if it is small it may discourage some. Remember, most people think you are doing better than you are. Let them continue to think so.

Another no-no, is telling people that the majority of your business is in one leg then identifying who the leader in that leg is. By doing this you are weakening your grip on the group. My rationale would be that if one person is so much of your business, then I want to follow that person, not you.

There is only one litmus test for determining leadership that is to have an organization where more than one leg is doing well. This means that the focal point in the leadership equation is the person at the apex of the width and depth spread.

Here then are the three things every good leader should do to maintain and grow a dynamic downline.

1. *Reassess your position daily*

Take stock of your progress. "Goals in concrete, plans in sand." Everyone knows that the best laid plans go awry. Stay in touch with the key leaders down in your depth as to their particular progress during the month. This means discussing volume, recruiting, and general attitude. I am amazed at the number of people who don't know where they're at as the end of the month draws near.

My upline always said that the last week's orders ought to equal or exceed the first three weeks combined!!!!! If you're paying attention, promoting the pin system, and have a great event coming up, your volume will explode at the end of each month. Finish every month with a flourish! Have a month end strategy cooked up every month.

Take inventory of your assets daily. You can't use something you haven't got. Knowing how much tool flow you have, will give you a feel for future growth. If you moved one hundred books of a certain title last month, then set a goal to increase that number this month. Incidentally, everyone should have one book that is recommended to each newcomer in the group. This is a vital tracking device for growth. (Naturally I recommend my first book "Raising a Giant")

2. Renew Your Perspective

Keep the group excited by keeping the dream alive at all times. Don't just tell them once, but tell them over and over again where the group is going. Book a larger meeting facility than ever before, and then challenge the leaders to fill it up! If I lived in Los Angeles, I would take my top ten or so leaders to lunch on Rodeo Drive, then after lunch I would take them all down to the Shrine Auditorium (Where they have the Academy Awards), and go inside and have them stand on the stage looking out at the seven thousand empty seats and imagine how big their incomes will be when we fill it up.

Think of the dreams that will come true when the sight of the Academy Awards becomes the site where they are recognized for their accomplishments! I can attest to the fact that standing on that stage, where I've seen so many movie stars and performers perform is an experience like no other!

When the group is going slow and getting discouraged, it is time for a new perspective. Be an idealist. Don't believe the "Be reasonable" crowd. Be unreasonable, what has being reasonable ever gotten you? Helen Keller was deaf and blind but graduated Magna Cum Laude from Radcliff University with a degree in English, a language she had never heard or seen! Unreasonable! Milton wrote poetry and was blind; Beethoven composed the entire "Fifth Symphony" after he was deaf! Emerson said, "Do the thing, and you shall have the power."

If a leader is to keep his/her long term perspective, he/she has to step back from the present.

3. *Resolve to press on*

Adversity is a part of the game. Some leaders are overcome by adversity, others build on it! I have noticed that the really great leaders love a good fight. They look for a reason to rile up the group. If you don't have an excited group, then create a crisis. Remember, all leaders live with opposition.

The daily grind gets to most people. They can see the dream only as long as there is little in the way. The role of the dynamic leader is to see the vision daily and to communicate to the entire group that the objective is to win every day.

Vince Lombardi, the fabled coach of the Green Bay Packers, once said, "You don't play well some of the time, you play well all of the time; you don't give your best some of the time, you give your best all of the time," Great advice.

Your group will sit down if you let them, they will quit if you let them, they will slow down if you let them, and they will die if you let them. Don't let them quit, or fail, or roll over and play dead. Your dream, your vision, your determination, your leadership will lead them to victory lane. Quit looking for a leader and become one today. Make a difference, you can you know!

Chapter 21

TESTED TRIED TRUE

"My attitude must be superior to those I lead."

\- Crisp's Second Law

If you take a chain and hold one end of it off the floor you will only move the amount of chain lifted. The rest of the chain lies dormant, inert on the floor in front of you. Now the part lying on the floor is just as strong as that which is dangling from your hand, but it is not being utilized. The same is true of a network marketing group. When the leader doesn't hold the entire organization to a standard, the standard of performance will suffer.

Most people engage in "tension relieving" activities rather than goal "achieving ones." After an exciting event, when they return to their "normal" lives, the daily drudgery still exists, and the negative tensions haven't gone away. It's called "Avoidance" and I don't recommend it.

One of my favorite all time movies starred Steve McQueen and Faye Dunnaway. It was called "The Thomas Crown Affair." The title song was called "Windmills of The Mind" and the lyrics said, "Like a circle in a spiral, like a wheel within a wheel, never ending or beginning in an ever-spinning reel, like the circles that you find in the windmills of your mind." Most lives go in circles. Network marketing leaders often find themselves going in circles. "Replacing" more than "advancing."

In the movie "Ground Hog Day;" Bill Murray wakes up every day to find that it is the same day. He relives the same day over and over again. His life is like a metronome, replaying the events of the day before. To stop the train and get off requires an interruption of patterns and routines. This "interruption" causes tension and shakes things up.

When I need a really good outline for whipping the group into shape, I rely on an old standby. Action, Creates, Tension. The acronym A C T!

No tension - there is no expectancy

No tension - there is no excitement

No tension - there is no sense of urgency

No tension - there is no adventure

No tension - there is no direction

No tension - there is no criticism from average people

No tension - there is no pride in accomplishment

No tension - there can be no winning

No tension - there is no reward

No tension - there is no need to dream

How do you create productive tension in the group? First, you must redefine what constitutes BIG! Most of us grow up with an idea of what we think big is. Big is someone taller than us, someone with more money than us, more fame, more material things, a bigger house, car, or better clothes.

The problem with most adults is that they continue to hold the same perspective of what big is. Twenty years later the school-yard bully is still pushing you around. Even though he has proven in his adult life that he is insignificant, he is still the standard by which you are measuring your own toughness, or skills, or abilities.

No one gets better if they are one of the links lying on the floor. Most people are waiting for someone to come along and whip the schoolyard bully, pick us up, and dust us off, and put us on the road to success. No one else will provide a tension filled, productive environment for us to prosper in. No one prospers in a vacuum!

In school, the tension came from deadlines for homework to be turned in, the Friday Quiz, and the infamous Finals.

Since school, we have not had to live with deadlines except when others (employers/bosses) made them for us. Now you're in charge of the deadlines. Create your own; you'll be amazed at the results.

In Irwin Shaw's novel "The Top of The Hill," the main character works for a very large Fortune 500 type company. He is the heir apparent to the job of Chief Executive Officer. He interrupts a closed board meeting to resign. In the next scene he is setting in a bar with his best friend, who also happens to work for the company, the friend asked, "Why did you do it?" Our hero replies, "I found myself trading ninety percent of what I didn't want to do, for ten percent of what I wanted to do." Later in the novel he tells a man who is dying "That a dream is the confirmation of life."

Tension, the right kind of tension, is life giving... confirming our existence, but only when it is focused on the process of getting what we really want out of life. Today, many are going through the motions of getting what they want. But the tension which underlies their existence is in the knowledge that what they are doing is spinning their lives out of control. That the pathway they are on will not lead them where they want to go. This kind of tension is a killer.

What is needed is tension that focuses on the "want to." People who are headed toward their "Want to" are less likely to shirk from the tensions of performance, but will instead take on the challenge with delight!

We also must redefine what FAST is, not as in "Not Eating" but as in "How fast does that car go?" The issue here is a sense of urgency! One of the most important things you can do is create a sense of immediacy in your group. This means "majoring in the majors," not "majoring in the minors."

As baby-boomers age, they are growing more and more discontent with the status quo. These are people who grew their hair long, experimented with psychedelic drugs, dropped out of mainstream society, and claimed to be "Society's Children." Many fought in Viet Nam, while others demonstrated and protested. All wanted freedom more than anything.

Many boomers children have grown up, left home, and now the boomers can visualize their freedom again.

The problem? No economic exit strategy. Network marketing offers them the way out. However, there is a catch. Most are not willing to get into something that will take ten to twenty years to build. By then they will be too old to enjoy the freedom.

The answer is to redefine what fast means. How fast can someone hope to build a good income from your business? The answer may lie with you. Are you kicking back, slowing down, got yours, don't care who gets theirs? Or are you revving up, charging the mountain and generally "On far?"

The key to success today may lie with your ability to convince others that you are serious about what you are doing and that you either have the answers, or know where to get the answers necessary to see them through to success. At best you have probably two to five years to help them reach their financial goals, and probably two to four months to convince your better members that their future is best served by being with you and your company.

It is not only important to convince people that your products are good and a value at the price you sell them for, but you must be able to convince them of your own competence and connections to upline help. This is why "The System" is so vital.

Actions create tensions. Positive dynamic tension is what it's all about. I think we all agree that lethargy is a killer. Don't be afraid to make waves. I had to move my sponsor aside in order to rise at the pace I needed to, to make my family financially secure. He had a baseball pension and enough resources to make it without getting in a hurry. I did not.

Of course you always run the risk of turning some people off (I did) because they think you're being too pushy. Better to be known as a "pusher" than to be known as a "slacker" or "lethargic leader," don't you think?

Your ability to lead will be tested over and over again, your ambitions challenged, and your integrity questioned. You will be tried, but you must remember that no one ever got better in a vacuum. This "testing and trying" is designed to get at the real issue which is being found "True." Without the fires of testing, the impurities would not be purged, and the truth would never emerge.

Loyalty and honor inspire trust. Unfortunately, this industry is not known for its loyalty. Most people are loyal to the buck. They don't understand the commitments that many have made to put them where they are. When you get together, talk about how your company is the best, your products excel, and how your line of sponsorship is number one!

When talking to people with other companies, brag on their company and encourage them to continue. If they aren't happy there, they will come to you eventually anyway, but you will have raised the level of integrity for everyone in the industry.

A defeatist spirit creates cowardly behavior, and engenders a dog eat dog environment. Yours is a volunteer army. No bosses, no rules against quitting, or going AWOL.

If you have to "fence" your group in then they're not yours to begin with. You protect best by giving them the answers to their important questions and by giving them an example to follow.

From the movie "Rob Roy" I gleaned this statement of value, "Honor is a gift a man gives himself and none can give it to him nor take it from him."

Sure Action Creates Tension, but the alternative is to allow the corrupt and overpowering influences of failure to prevail. Don't run away, step up and be counted. If you give up small beliefs, give up pretense, and give up comfortable traditions. You can get what you want!

Chapter 22

THE BIG THREE NEVERS

"There is no medicine for the life that fled."

-- Emerson

In contradiction to the sage advice to "Never say never," probably penned by that famous philosopher "Anonymous," I want to share with you three "Nevers." For the most part they are common sense things that most people would do naturally, however adhering to the admonition to "Never take anything for granted," I will share the Big Three with you now.

1. Never promise more than you can or are willing to give!

Nothing is more debilitating than having someone promise one thing and deliver much less. In this world though, it seems to be a fact of life that some people have to promise the moon in order to get us to buy their products or participate in their schemes. This is especially true when you are working in depth.

Working in depth requires that you move through the downline quickly. The perception may be easy to leave that you are going to do a lot more hand-holding than is possible.

Don't leave the impression that you are going to do everything for someone! Working depth means driving the leg "downward," not spending a good deal of time working "width in depth."

Make sure to deliver more than you promised and press this concept throughout the downline. Plugging people into "The System" will alleviate a lot of the perceived of lack of help. When initially training new people be certain to tell them what to expect. Don't sugar coat it because most of us don't "get it" when "It" is obscured by candy-coating.

2. *Never give less than your best!*

One of the reasons, I believe, for my tremendous success in network marketing is that I always gave one hundred percent, even when it was not easy to do.

I recently was booked to do a seminar for 500 to 1000 people in Kansas City. I arrived at the hotel meeting room to find a crowd of 35. At great expense I had trusted an agent to deliver the bodies. He failed, but I had 35 brave souls who had paid the fee and expected to get fed. I did what I always do. I acted like a professional and reached down inside and gave them a seminar to remember. I have received many thank you notes from those in attendance.

I learned this from the world renowned Zig Ziglar early in my career. He made a special effort to come speak to a crowd of "300 plus" (That I was to deliver) that turned out to be a dozen including myself. For years now I've called this my "Fiasco at North Park." It was embarrassing to say the least. When I tried to pay Zig, he refused and said, "It was on him." Zig did a great job and I have never forgotten.

What goes around does indeed come around. When you don't give your best, it is reflected in the group. Soon attendance at meetings will fall, people will stop buying products, and your credibility will be shot.

When I walk in I want everyone to pay attention. I dress the part, act the part, and speak the part. The leader never leaves anything up to chance; the better you plan, the better the performance.

I can't figure out why people who don't give their very best are always surprised when they don't get the results they wanted. They sow the seeds of mediocrity then pray for a crop failure. Excuses abound with these people. It's always someone else's fault.

The girl that can't dance... says the band can't play.

We must not forget that we are dealing with other people's lives. There is much at stake. Children with crooked teeth who need orthodontics, mothers who need to stay home and raise their young, mothers and fathers who need to be free from an oppressive boss. There are dreams to be dreamed and songs to be sung. Don't let lackadaisical performance cause you to let yourself and others down. There is never an acceptable excuse for giving less than your very best!

3. **Never give up and never give in!**

It is so easy to live negatively. The world around us is focused on the bad and defeat is an accepted way of life. Building a network marketing business requires dealing with enough negative. It is imperative to focus your ideas and actions on positives, to be "solution," not "problem" oriented.

The reason most people quit is that they fail to see a viable way out. They cannot conceive of sponsoring a large enough downline to create an income they find significant.

Tenacity and toughness are taught. Those who persist win! The wolves are always out there prowling around for strays, preying on the unsuspecting and weak. It is true that a smooth sea never made a good sailor!

Building a giant downline means keeping your new emerging leaders focused on the road ahead. Never quit teaching the "Nevers."

This means in weekly meetings you indoctrinate "The Nevers."

At monthly awards meetings you preach "The Nevers."

In newsletters address "The Nevers."

Never promise more than you can or are willing to give.

Never give anything but your best.

Never give up or give in.

CHAPTER 23

THE GREAT MIGRATION

"If one man can change the world, shouldn't everyone try?" –John Kennedy

After THIRTY years in the network marketing world I have come to the conclusion that the more things change the more they remain the same.

Though the industry is changing rapidly, the fact is that people are people regardless of the era in which they live. As we move into new millennium it pays to look back and learn, as well as ahead and plan.

Change is inevitable. Competition is stiffer. The better the competition, the more imperative it is to study and work harder. Leadership in the new millennium will come from those who just now are getting their first taste of network marketing success.

In the past, successful companies have been "cult like" in their approach. The future may find a more logical "business like" approach being used. The two may not be as incompatible as some think.

Books such as "The Third Wave" have heralded the changing times in which we as network marketers live. Paul

Zane Pilzer introduced the world to a new "Distribution Model" involving the distribution of information, or as he calls it "Intellectual Distribution." The advent of cell phones with cameras and emarketing, telemarketing, conference calls, and the Internet have certainly presented some new mediums for us to use to build the basic structure of a downline.

Some, caught up in "Third Wave" thinking have ignored some time tested principles of dealing with people. Particularly "groups" of people. Relationship building has been put on the back burner, replaced by heal-you-in-a-minute get rich quick schemes that promise much and deliver little.

If you asked the roughly twenty five million people who are involved in the network marketing world today what the biggest weakness in their company is, they would rise up in chorus and say "Sponsoring Support System." They are going to be wowed by the new internet options available from companies such as www.allaxismedia.com.

One of the leading advocates of building "mail-order" downlines, has recently recanted his bold position of recent years by declaring that "I built a downline of over 70,000 by mailings and couldn't get them to do anything."

Today he goes about preaching the gospel of building relationships through events, recognition, and proper preparation. A theme that has been proclaimed loudly by my former mentor Dexter Yager, and myself, and a host of others. People still fall for the shortcuts and then complain when they don't produce the expected results.

Internet Note:

The internet has become a warm fuzzy way to communicate. Video email and high speed internet connections have enabled an old technology to be deployed in a new and inexpensive way.

The sheer numbers of participants in network marketing have become staggering! The network marketing industry may have more actual participants than any other type of industry or movement in the world! More than computers, more than oil, more than transportation, more than electronics!

The rapid rise in active participants has created some new and interesting opportunities. Like most opportunities, this one surfaced out of need. Lacking today is a well trained and capable leadership force to stabilize businesses, and mobilize downlines for continued growth. What we are now seeing is a "migration" of participants from one company to the next.

This massive migrating herd of people is not the same as the ones that we saw a decade ago. This one, besides being larger, is much more focused, vocal, independent, and less patient.

This is an activist crowd. Baby-Boomers and Generation Xers and of course the "GenNext" crowd of young entrepreneurs that have little regard for broken promises and nonperformance! This group is susceptible like those in the past to the unique and absurd, but is too savvy to be deceived for long.

Their overall attitude is "I'm going to give you 90 to 120 days to prove to me that you can and will deliver on your promises, if not, there are plenty of other opportunities awaiting."

Never have I seen the "Ground Floor" mentality so prevalent. A significant number of these people have tried network marketing before. Old line companies such as Amway, Shaklee and Herbalife have gone through millions of participants. Someone recently guessed that fully one-third of Amway's present recruits are "retreads." Those who are going back to where they started. They are doing so because they are tired of fly-by-night deals, body brokers, and scam artists. They are returning to a reliable standard.

Rich DeVos, Amway Co-Founder, told me personally over twenty-five years ago that for the most part, the network marketing crowd was a "Passing Parade." I believe that to be true. Today, I believe that more than half of the people attending opportunity meetings are simply "Checking out the competition" and "Thinking about making a change." In the next few years, more than half of the participants today will change companies.

These are not what we commonly referred to in the past as "network marketing junkies," but many are alert business men and women who are simply "doing research" and their "inside due diligence" while searching for the right opportunity.

Since it doesn't require a large investment to do so, it makes sense to just get in, look around, ask questions, give it a go, and see what happens. The general attitude is "so what if the company folds or my upline fails to deliver support? I can change companies in a heartbeat." And they do.

What are they looking for? How can you stop the bleeding, turn the tide, retain more? The answers are not so simple. I have tried to address many of them. People are looking for truth. For a company AND upline who really deliver on their promises. Most are willing to learn and work, but they see themselves as running out of time. Boomers are ready to slow down, to kick back and enjoy life. Generation Xers and GenNexters are eager, idealistic, and bold!

The 75 million baby-boomers had 72 million children! These young men and women are graduating high school and college, thinking about their futures, and anxious to get on with their lives. They are also not as starry eyed as previous generations were about the life as a corporate employee. They've seen downsizing for themselves. Watched as their parents fought the workaday world and they are not so certain they want to get caught in the same trap.

These two groups of people are complemented by a group in the middle who are just beginning to have a family. This group has some serious challenges too. In the United States alone they tell me there are over 4 million birth mothers each year! Consider that you double that number when you add dad into the equation, now you have 8 million! You can multiply by four to add grandparents into the mix, and now you have in the neighborhood of 40 million parents and grandparents directly involved with newborns every year!

If you expand the group to include those from birth through three, toddler age, you now have 70 - 100 million people with babies or grandbabies!

What does all this mean to the savvy network marketer? Simple. Boomers need money to slow down and live the good life. "Generation Xers and Nexters" need money to avoid the trap their parents fell into. Those in the middle are dealing with expanding expenses and potentially lower incomes, as working mothers wrestle with whether to turn their precious newborns over to strangers to raise.

What with disease, child abuse issues, and education, this new mother may not be as quick to go back to work as she once might have been. She may be more likely to look at a way to earn income while staying at home. Families are looking for options.

The old traditional opportunity meeting time of 7 - 8 PM may not suit her new responsibilities. She is available between 10 AM and 2 PM for business meetings (held in her home or in a home where childcare is provided). She's more apt to go for more formal "coffees, afternoon teas," and "get - togethers." The company that taps into this market will do well indeed.

While I believe it is impossible to stop the migration, it is very possible to slow it down. To bring about a slower attrition rate, one must consider why people leave. Being treated like a number, or ignored by your upline, is a surefire way to assure a higher attrition rate. Eye to eye, and belly to belly, relationship building will win the day. (As it always has.)

More dynamic and effective personal development programs, followed by powerful and in depth network marketing leadership development programs are essential.

Ask yourself what kind of people do you want in your business? Then ask what you think those kind of people are looking for? What do they respond to? Are they likely to buy a "get rich quick scheme" presented by a massive email system or blast? Or are they more apt to be impressed with a well thought out presentation and game plan for on-going success?

The migration will continue. As more companies fail, and are replaced by still yet more companies, the speed at which the migration accelerates is anyone's guess. One thing is for certain, "the cream will rise to the top."

To find yourself on the success side of the fence take a moment to ask some critical questions. Am I a drifter or am I a seeker? If you are a drifter, you'll likely go a long way, you just won't get far. Does your present company and upline offer you the three necessary "System" driven support elements?

1. An effective and well coordinated Event System augmented by effective webinars and podcasts

2. A logical and well designed recognition program supplemented by a dynamic web recognition system (One that fits with the bonus plan)

3. Tools, Training, and Leadership Development monitored and tracked by sophisticated web-based software

I firmly believe the past has proven the wisdom of finding a company and sticking with it. The grass may appear greener but it rarely is. Leaving one company to go to the next usually is an exercise in futility. There are, I suppose, extenuating circumstances. I've run into some seedy people in this business and wouldn't want to find myself in their downline for anything.

Choose wisely, find a good company and dig in. Make a fanatical start, stay focused, and don't drift. Feed yourself and your organization food that nourishes "Giants" daily.

"Seek, and you shall find." Be a seeker. Keep an open mind. Embrace an all out attitude and second to none work ethic. All of your dreams can come true! The dreamer builder is you!

This is the most exciting journey you'll ever take, make it fun, give your best... don't save your best!

Thanks for telling others if you like my book, and if you didn't, keep it to yourself.

I gotta go now, it's meeting time, and someone out there is gonna see the opportunity again tonight... Lucky dogs.

Internet Summary

Those resistant to change are doomed. The internet offers even the smallest person the chance to be BIG. This highway runs from your home or office into millions even billions of homes, offices, mobile phones. Social networks like myspace.com, facebook, Plaxo, linkedin.com, and twitter.com have changed the face of human interaction forever.

If you're stuck in the past and refuse to come onboard this speeding train then you are going to go the way of the dinosaurs. It amazes me how many companies have failed to embrace the cutting edge technology of emarketing. They failed to recognize that Amway and Avon, two of the biggest companies in direct-selling adopted the internet a decade ago.

Websites for most companies fail to offer database collection and a way sort prospects from customers from new distributors. Email… a cheap and efficient way to reach out to everyone with a message of thanks, hope, and opportunity… is left to chance.

I talk to hundreds of networkers weekly and am stunned by their ignorance of the available and affordable internet solutions.

So I took matters into my own hands and developed one of the most complete emarketing solutions ever. Activated by simple to use software you can now attract the best and brightest to your team… without leaving home you can attend the best network marketing training courses… collect data on thousands of potential customers and affiliates.

You can build professional websites and web-based communications tools to fit your needs. You can capture leads and lists from new distributor's address books… you can use soft email approaches so as not to violate spam laws and find out who out there REALLY is looking for the "RIGHT" opportunity…

As an American Senior (According to the Denny's breakfast menu) I am "Hip" to the new net… I am fascinated by the vast reach of this wonderful tool. I love webcasts, blogs, noozles, tweating, webinars, conference calls, facebook, myspace, youtube, and video email…

The internet offers a powerful way to leverage your time and financial resources. Why talk to one when you can talk to thousands or even millions? And probably do it more affectively than face-to-face.

Does this mean abandon all the old ways? Absolutely not… instead of a "list" we now have an email address book… our goals still need to be set, and events take on a whole new meaning if not style… Blockbuster didn't kill the movie industry… it only enhanced it.

If you're upline and company are up to speed… then I recommend you use their systems… if not, if you are disappointed, or just want to find out what "else" is available… please take a look at one of my websites… www.gobobcrisp.com or blog at www.gocrispblog.com or www.allaxismedia.com.

THOUGHTS & TRIBUTES

To all the many who have encouraged me along the way… the numbers are too many to count… but my gratitude is also endless. As I have aged I have grown to love network marketing even more. Sure, we have our rogues, mavericks, crooks and clowns but what industry doesn't? Space simply wouldn't allow me to enumerate the many things each of the following people has meant to my growth, both personally and professionally.

My parents Ken and Len Crisp neither of whom graduated from high school but both found their genius in life. My kids Candace, Julie and Jeremy and Cindy and Stephanie. Joni Locht, Roger and Cathy Blake, Dexter Yager, Rick Setzer, Bill Britt, Dr. Tom Payne. My first mentor Warren Gray who taught me how to learn and to be curious about all things in life.

Gary Hines who gave me "The Magic of Thinking Big" and believed in me when few did… Pat Yamada, Dr. Vince Thomas best friends for 30+ years and Vince's wife Diana who is perhaps the kindest person I ever met…

The mother of my children Jo Crisp who was a mainstay in my first network marketing endeavor and who played such an integral role in raising our GREAT children.

To Rich DeVos of Amway fame who I still think of as my second father. New friends Adam Packard and Rob & Carole Crisp and Jeff and Sam Higginson, Glen Jensen, Craig Bradley, Joe Cutler, Carsten Werner and his wife

Ingrid. Gary and Sherry Windfield who have shared so many great times with me… Great industry leaders who are too many to number… all deserve my thanks.

And to the future… my young grandchildren that include Montana, Kendall, Regan, Lincoln, and Luke… my hope is to do my part to make it a better world… with cleaner air to breathe, better schools, more opportunities, and a generally happier and healthier environment to live and prosper in.

Too many people still die of cancer and heart disease… hopefully the best minds of this century will find a cure soon. Let's all support the causes the make people more aware than ever. Let's get involved BIG in the effort to change hatefulness to love, war for peace, disease for healing and prevention, and let's celebrate life everyday… it beats the alternative.

A tribute here to the men who fight for freedom all over the world and for those who fought and died we utter a prayer of thanks and thanksgiving for the price they paid for us to be able to exercise these rights we enjoy… to America the greatest nation in the world even with all her flaws.